Measurement Trends in Career and Vocational Education

Ronald C. Rodgers, *Editor*

NEW DIRECTIONS FOR TESTING AND MEASUREMENT
Jayjia Hsia, *Consulting Editor*

Number 20, December 1983

Paperback sourcebooks in
The Jossey-Bass Social and Behavioral Science Series

Jossey-Bass Inc., Publishers
San Francisco • Washington • London

Ronald C. Rodgers (Ed.)
Measurement Trends in Career and Vocational Education.
New Directions for Testing and Measurement, no. 20.
San Francisco: Jossey-Bass, 1983.

New Directions for Testing and Measurement Series
Michael Kean, *Editor-in-Chief*

New Directions for Testing and Measurement is published
quarterly by Jossey-Bass Inc., Publishers. Subscriptions, single-issue
orders, change of address notices, undelivered copies, and other
correspondence should be sent to Journal Subscriptions, Jossey-Bass Inc.,
Publishers, 433 California Street, San Francisco, California 94104.

Library of Congress Catalogue Card Number LC 83-82853
International Standard Serial Number ISSN 0271-0609
International Standard Book Number ISBN 87589-976-5

Cover art by Willi Baum
Manufactured in the United States of America

Ordering Information

The paperback sourcebooks listed below are published quarterly and can be ordered by single-copy.

Single copies are available at $9.95 when payment accompanies order, and *all single-copy orders under $25.00 must include payment.* (California, New Jersey, New York, and Washington, D.C., residents please include appropriate sales tax.) For billed orders, cost per copy is $9.95 plus postage and handling. (Prices subject to change without notice.)

Bulk orders (ten or more copies) of any individual sourcebook are available at the following discounted prices: 10–49 copies, $8.95 each; 50–100 copies, $7.95 each; over 100 copies, *inquire.* Sales tax and postage and handling charges apply as for single copy orders.

To ensure correct and prompt delivery, all orders must give either the *name of an individual* or an *official purchase order number.* Please submit your order as follows:

Subscriptions: specify series and year subscription is to begin.
Single Copies: specify sourcebook code (such as, TM8) and first two words of title.

Mail orders for United States and Possessions, Latin America, Canada, Japan, Australia, and New Zealand to:
Jossey-Bass Inc., Publishers
433 California Street
San Francisco, California 94104

Mail orders for all other parts of the world to:
Jossey-Bass Limited
28 Banner Street
London EC1Y 8QE

New Directions for Testing and Measurement Series
Michael Kean, *Editor-in-Chief*

Contents

Editor's Notes

One of the greatest challenges for anyone who tries to help others to select, prepare for, and succeed in the labor markets of 1984 and beyond lies in coping with the abundance of information, opportunities, and uncertainty surrounding decisions about work today. On the one hand, there is far too much information to absorb about occupations for anyone to consider or try them all. On the other hand, much of the information that is available is too unstable, complex, or fragmented to answer the most important question facing the job-seeking individual: namely, how can I find a job I like that lets me live where and in a way I want?

These challenges are complicated by the rate and extent of economic and political change in world, national, and local labor markets. The unpredictability and controversy surrounding worldwide energy shortages and surpluses, monetary exchange rates, trade imbalances, and rapidly developing technology can trigger shifts in jobs throughout the world. All these events are far beyond the control of the individual counselor, teacher, parent, teenager, or adult who faces the challenge of choosing an occupation today.

Fifty years ago, most people faced easier choices. A person was most likely to enter an occupation closely related to that of his or her parents. Simple economics narrowed the range of choices for people who could not afford college. Technology and transportation kept most jobs immobile, so the risk that employers would shift thousands of jobs from one region of the country to another was extremely small. Two world wars and economic depression helped to define job satisfaction as doing any job well so that one could not only earn a living but could contribute to the welfare of the nation as well.

Many of today's workers — especially those born after 1945 — arrived on the job with a different set of values and expectations. The prosperity of the 1950s and 1960s convinced many that the welfare of the nation was assured. Today, many assume that everyone should be entitled to a personally satisfying, well-paying job. That honorable concept made its way into much of the employment and training legislation and policy after 1945. Unfortunately, many jobs are neither personally satisfying nor well paying. These two factors alone can seldom survive very long as the primary criteria for judging most jobs. In most cases, they are incentives that require trade-offs among factors on opposite ends of a continuum.

Technology and television increased expectations that personal fortunes and a comfortable life are more the result of luck than of patient, persistent effort over many years. Boundaries between reality and entertaining fantasy have been blurred. People who worked hard to achieve their own

1

success were astonished when their children wanted to skip the hard work and move directly to fame and fortune. Unfortunately, no guaranteed formulas for fame, fortune, and lifelong job satisfaction exist, nor is there any evidence that they will exist soon, despite widespread interest in easy ways to success.

Education also appears to have increased these expectations. Community colleges and federal aid programs have brought postsecondary education into virtually everyone's range of choices and opportunities. Meanwhile, graduate training has created a situation in which M.B.A.'s can receive offers of more than $30,000 per year for their first job while the oversupply in certain other markets forces capable, hard-working Ph.D.'s to take any job they can find because demand for the skills that they invested years in refining is low.

This portrayal is not intended to be a nostalgic wish for the time when occupational choices were easier to make: That is not only impossible, but it offers many disadvantages as well. However, it may be helpful to consider how changes have altered the climate in which teenagers and adults must make career decisions in 1984 and beyond. The questions for my three-year-old son and his peers will be more radical still. He will never know a time without microwave ovens and home computers. Future changes in technology may radically alter the type of preparation that he and his peers need in order to enter and succeed in the occupations of the next century. That is likely to be a topic for future volumes of this and other journals over the next two decades.

As a result of these changes, the need to select, prepare for, and enter an occupation has become extremely complex and potentially frightening. Occupational choice has become a burden that can leave an otherwise confident, capable person fragmented and confused. What does that suggest for a person who is less confident or capable? Few people are certain where and how their talents and interests can fit into the labor markets of 1984 and beyond.

Fortunately, the environment that spawned the complexity has also created new insights and resources to help counselors, teachers, parents, teenagers, and adults cope with the burdens of occupational choice. The purpose of this *New Directions for Testing and Measurement* sourcebook is to offer clues and recommendations that can add to these resources and insights, especially for those who try to help others to make these difficult decisions. Each chapter examines and recommends resources that can improve the quality of occupational choices in 1984 and beyond. The first three chapters focus on practical lessons from the experience of school practitioners, strategies for linking labor market information with training and education, and efforts to define, measure, and facilitate work adjustment. The next three chapters examine special needs and resources for serving handicapped persons, the impact of computers on counseling and guidance, and the role of measurement in occupations in which licensing, certification, and regulation control entry and success. Each chapter concludes with recommendations for future thinking, measurement, and research that can improve the quality and integration of resources available to help teenagers and adults select, prepare for, and succeed in occupations throughout their lives.

In Chapter One, Mastie relies on the practical experience and accumulated wisdom of elementary and secondary schools to consider present and future needs and resources for those concerned about vocational choice and career development in the schools. Her goal is to offer as many how-to suggestions and examples of appropriate use of new and needed resources as she can to enhance the payoff to individual students, teachers, and counselors.

In Chapter Two, Cassell and Rodgers examine the link between labor market information and training and education. They begin by considering the role of information and counselors in the labor market. After proposing ways of responding to the limitations of available information about jobs, they offer a model that enables a person to enter training with a prescriptive view of how his or her skills, experience, interests, and needs match local and national labor market opportunities.

In Chapter Three, Campbell considers the recurrent challenges of work adjustment as a person enters a new occupation or organization. The model that he proposes for analyzing the internal labor market might well serve as a blueprint for thinking about how better to serve the unemployed as well as a way of confronting the challenges that face the person who changes jobs.

In Chapter Four, Kapes and Parrish consider the career development and decision-making needs of handicapped individuals. They begin by clarifying the definition of handicapped, then make some recommendations for using career guidance and assessment tools responsive to the special needs of handicapped individuals. They also include a comprehensive summary of instruments and resources available to assist in educational placement and training.

In Chapter Five, Harris-Bowlsbey examines the implications and opportunities emerging from computer-assisted occupational information and guidance systems. She begins with an excellent analysis of the elements of systematic career guidance and the environment in which computers and other career-related resources can be used effectively. She then considers the impact of computers on vocational assessment and counseling practices for individuals, counselors, administrators, and test and system developers.

In Chapter Six, the Nowakowskis and Lane break new ground with an analysis of the role of measurement in accounting, law, and medicine. Their detailed examination across these three professions offers profound and provocative insights into entry-level and performance barriers in all occupations that rely on certification, licensing, and regulation to influence performance, ethics, and training. Their observations should stimulate much new thinking about what counselors need to know as they help those considering entry into these occupations.

This volume is exploratory in nature. Each chapter assesses the state of the art in its particular area. Many other areas could have been addressed, but time and space were limited. Thus, much recent work in vocational measurement and occupational guidance is not reflected here. Nevertheless, if these chapters serve to catalyze further thinking, measurement, and research of value to practitioners, this *New Directions* sourcebook will have served its purpose well.

Ronald C. Rodgers
Editor

Ronald C. Rodgers is an assistant director of the Midwestern
Field Service Office of the Educational Testing Service
in Evanston, Illinois.

*Help is available for counseling and career education practitioners
who need information about present and future capabilities of
career guidance measures.*

Career Guidance and Testing:
What Practitioners Need to Know

Marjorie M. Mastie

All the contributors to this volume and probably most of its readers as well are
comfortably situated in support roles well behind the front lines of American
education. As consultants, counselor educators, test developers, researchers,
program administrators, or resource publishers, it is easy for us to lose sight of
the practitioners who implement our theories, teach from our workbooks,
interpret our tests, and apply our recommendations. Thus, this chapter asks,
What do busy counselors and career educators need to know as they move into
the next decade? How can we provide it in the practical form that they demand?

What Do Students Need?

This section begins with an overview of our understanding of the career
development of young people of school age. Specific developmental tasks for
each age will be cited. Selected findings from the National Assessment of Educational Progress (NAEP) and the Michigan Educational Assessment Program (MEAP) will provide insights into where we are and how we are doing.

R. C. Rodgers (Ed.). *Measurement Trends in Career and Vocational Education.* New Directions
for Testing and Measurement, no. 20. San Francisco: Jossey-Bass, December 1983.

Basic Principles of Career Development. Although any number of theoretical formulations from the work of the leaders in career guidance could be provided here, the distillation that follows is a favorite with practitioners.

First, career development is an ongoing process, a series of choices. An individual makes choices throughout his or her life span as both the individual and the environment change. The individual will be changed as surely by education, experiences, opportunities, personal contacts, and allegiances as the environment will be changed by technological and sociological progress. Keeping in touch with these changes, both individual and environmental, and keeping these changes in sync will be crucial.

Second, decision making and planning are processes that can be learned and applied throughout the life span. Identifying a problem, gathering information, generating alternatives, weighing options, and designing action plans are all steps that can be taught in the early elementary grades and reinforced throughout the subsequent years of schooling. In this way, individuals can be encouraged and trained to take responsibility for their own lives, which will prepare them to cope with developmental changes and the choices ahead.

Third, multiple self factors are involved in career choices. These factors include interests, aptitudes, achievement, skills, needs, values, and self-concept. The subjective factors are especially influential. Decision making improves as the individual's understanding of these factors grows. Both formal and informal appraisal techniques can improve a person's understanding of them.

Fourth, past experiences influence present needs and values. While past experiences are not irreversible, it is important to start where the individual is. Recognizing and accepting these experiences and their effects clears the way for movement beyond them.

Fifth, the social context influences present thinking. The expectations of peers, family, significant adults, and society at large can be identified for their impact on the individual's own thinking. This is particularly important where options that are nontraditional for the person's sex, ethnic group, age, handicap, or other factor are being rejected. Recognizing and accepting the limiting expectations clears the way for movement beyond them.

Sixth, the myth of the one right job is detrimental and inaccurate. Each individual can find success and satisfaction in a number of occupational and life role options. Acceptance of the range of potentially successful choices frees the individual for enlightened career decision making and planning for change. Today's young people must be told that those in their generation will average between four and nine jobs during their lifetime and that they must plan to acquire skills useful in a variety of employment opportunities and situations.

Seventh, self-concept and belief in self are of major importance. An individual will choose only the options that he or she feels capable of doing. The range of these possible options can be expanded significantly by trying out many roles and settings. We must encourage exploration in hobbies, studies, friends, and personal styles.

Eighth, luck can be prepared for but not depended on. Laboratory researchers believe that chance favors the prepared mind. The stronger the individual's background of self-understanding, developed skills, and acquired information, the greater the likelihood that he or she will successfully recognize and benefit from chance. Doing nothing while waiting for good fortune to happen assures that it probably will not. Preparation is essential if one is to be ready when an attractive opportunity presents itself. Timing and recognition are necessary if a person is to take advantage of good luck when it occurs.

Developmental Tasks of Career Development. The concept of developmental tasks has long proved useful in understanding and facilitating child development. This concept holds that there are necessary behaviors that all children must master, that these behaviors are acquired in sequential steps, and that the steps not taken create barriers to mastery, which can freeze the youngster at a particular stage of development.

Clearly, the idea of developmental tasks is as relevant to the career development of young people as it is to their learning to walk. It is simply not possible for students to arrive at age eighteen, look around, and say, "Ah ha! I am going to be a _____!" Much preparation is necessary, and the pattern of steps in which it must occur is almost as indispensable as the pattern necessary in learning other skills.

One significant attempt to define these developmental tasks in career development occurred in the performance objectives for nine-year-olds, thirteen-year-olds, seventeen-year-olds, and young adults aged twenty-six to thirty-five written over a decade ago for the National Assessment of Educational Progress (National Assessment of Educational Progress, 1971, p. 15). NAEP's career and occupational development objectives described each age span in several categories:

1. Prepare for making career decisions
   A. Know own characteristics relevant to career decisions
   B. Know the characteristics and requirements of different careers and occupations
   C. Relate own personal characteristics to occupational requirements
   D. Plan for career development of change
2. Improve career and occupational capabilities
3. Possess skills that are generally useful in the world of work
   A. Have generally useful numerical skills
   B. Have generally useful communication skills
   C. Have generally useful manual-perceptual skills
   D. Have generally useful information-processing and decision-making skills
   E. Have generally useful interpersonal skills
   F. Have employment-seeking skills

4. Practice effective work habits
   A. Assume responsibility for own behavior
   B. Plan work
   C. Use initiative and ingenuity to fulfill responsibilities
   D. Adapt to varied conditions
   E. Maintain good health and grooming
5. Have positive attitudes toward work
   A. Recognize the bases of various attitudes toward work
   B. Hold competence and excellence in high regard
   C. Seek personal fulfillment through own achievement
   D. Value work in terms of societal goals

Exercises were written at each age level to assess each objective. About 100,000 students completed the exercises in 1973-74 for the first nationwide assessment of career development. (Unfortunately, it is the only such assessment so far.) NAEP's objectives parallel the pioneering work of Frank Parson and his followers. The logical development of these constructs and their interrelationships are discussed by Cassell and Rodgers in Chapter Two.

Over the last decade, many states adopted their own assessments mirroring the NAEP model. Almost every statewide assessment measures reading and mathematics skills, but a variety of other subjects have also been included: science, writing, health education, music, citizenship and social studies, art, and—in a growing number of states—career development. For example, Michigan conducted its second statewide assessment of career development in grades 4, 7, and 10 in fall 1983. Michigan used results of its 1979 assessment to revise its career development objectives. These efforts have created still another description of the developmental tasks in this area (Michigan Educational Assessment Program, 1983, pp. 1-8):

Component #1: Self-Awareness and Assessment
(Who Am I Now?)

Grade 4 example: Identify some things that s/he is learning to do now that s/he was not able to do before

Grade 7 example: Examine those attitudes and work habits that enable one to succeed, and determine what s/he will do to attain these traits

Grade 10 example: Evaluate his/her growth in independence

Component #2: Career Awareness and Exploration
(What Can I Become?)

Grade 4 example: Identify tasks performed by people in the job cited

Grade 7 example: Identify nontraditional and traditional roles that men and women have in home, work, community, and leisure settings

Grade 10 example: Name a variety of career exploration activities in which s/he has participated

Component #3: Career Decision Making
(How Do I Decide What To Become?)

Grade 4 example: Recognize a variety of decisions s/he makes on
                   her/his own at home, in school, and with friends
Grade 7 example: Identify responsibilities that accompany the
                   decision
Grade 10 example: Indicate important factors to consider in making
                   the decision (including personal and external
                   factors)

Component #4: Career Planning and Placement
(How Do I Get There?)

Grade 4 example: Name people who could help with a cited problem
Grade 7 example: Describe a plan to solve a cited problem
Grade 10 example: Recognize personal, economic, and social reasons
                   for possible career changes throughout one's life

Iowa has developed a resource that can be implemented by local school districts without formal state assessments. Educational Testing Service (ETS) recently completed a three-year revision of the Iowa Career Education Inventory (Educational Testing Service, 1981) to measure career education objectives developed by teachers, counselors, and administrators. The Iowa inventory is designed to serve as a curriculum planning tool by assessing student mastery of career education concepts in grades 3, 6, 9, and 12 in seven domains (Rodgers, 1983): self, interpersonal relationships, self and society, decision making, economics, occupations knowledge, and work values and attitudes.

Thus, practitioners have several sources for career development objectives that they can use in building career education into curriculum planning. Many of these objectives have associated test items that are available for local curriculum evaluation, needs assessment, and the like. Some item sources also offer comparison data from national or other large-scale samples. Almost all have been jointly developed by practitioners and measurement experts. As a result, the objectives are not only realistic but psychometrically and statistically strong. Almost without exception, they elaborate observable, sequential behaviors across the elementary and secondary years. And, there is sufficient variation among them that any local district, project, or study should be able to locate a set that it can use as is or adapt to suit its particular needs.

Sample Findings. Practitioners need solid data that report what their students know and what they need to learn. Yet, consider the difference between the mathematics faculty in a high school and the career guidance and career education professionals. The former have access almost daily to clean, quantifiable data on their students' attainments. The latter often do not know until years after students' high school graduation whether they successfully made the initial transition to work. One of the few available sources of data for counselors over the years has been the annual report to the high schools from the American College Testing (ACT) program that summarizes students' reactions to their high school career guidance experiences. But, ACT examinees are not a cross section of the student population, and the data are frequently too global and too subjective for real program planning.

In contrast, data from the large-scale assessment projects can offer specific, practical assistance. For example, a five-volume series of interpretive analyses by guidance professionals examined data from the 1973–74 NAEP measures (Aubrey, 1978; Miller, 1978; Mitchell, 1978; Teideman and others, 1978; Westbrook, 1978). Four volumes are age-specific; the fifth volume looks at career development skills, understanding, and attitudes across the ages assessed — nine-, thirteen- and seventeen-year-old schoolchildren and young adults between the ages of twenty-six and thirty-five. These efforts yielded many valuable insights. For example, when asked to list ten different things that a person should think about in choosing a job or career, respondents showed increasing ability with age to list more things in all and subtler things (Teideman, 1978). Only 10 percent of the thirteen-year-olds could name any ten things; most concentrated on such mechanics as pay or working conditions and on personal satisfaction and interests. However, by age seventeen, 26 percent could name ten things, and 37 percent of the young adults could do so, with the older respondents adding such varied, subtle items as challenge (15 percent at seventeen), prestige (28 percent), possible discrimination (2 percent), and ethical considerations (3 percent). This steady progression in sensitivity to the issues involved in career decision making is promising.

Asked who should make the final decision about the kind of job that the child would take, 20 percent of the nine-year-olds responded that their parents should. This answer dropped to 7 percent at age thirteen and to 1 percent at age seventeen. The preferred response, *myself,* was selected by only 39 percent of the nine-year-olds, but it grew to 87 percent by age seventeen (Tiedeman, 1978). Here, too, the trend is promising. Moreover, the data should help to improve practice by focusing attention on this work attitude in particular.

Another attitudinal exercise from NAEP illustrates how data can clarify a very real need. Respondents at ages thirteen, seventeen, and twenty-six through thirty-five were asked to give six reasons why people who are willing to work can find it hard to get a good job. Responses were grouped as follows: age, race, sex, ethnic and religious discrimination, overqualification, police record, past drinking or drug problem, personality, manners, attitude, appearance, and other discriminatory practices. Twenty-six percent of the seventeen-year-olds cited age as a barrier. However, no other barrier was named by even 20 percent at any age, including the young adults, and several expected answers were ignored or named by fewer than 10 percent of the sample (Tiedeman, 1978). Thus, not only do young people appear to have little sensitivity to discriminatory hiring practices, but we appear to be doing little to improve the situation. Evidently, the attitude that a person finds work if he or she really wants to begins early, goes unchecked, and thrives among a majority of adults. To the degree that this makes our citizens unsympathetic to groups who are disproportionately unemployed or underemployed, this attitude is unfortunate. To the degree that it means that they will not fight for their own rights in the workplace, they have been shortchanged. The analysis by Cassell and Rodgers in Chapter Two reflects this pattern in conflicting pressures between "workfare" as a welfare substitute and declining federal and state support to help the long-term unemployed prepare for good jobs.

Obviously, the NAEP findings could be mined for numerous practical implications for the schools. However, there is considerable value for practitioners in the various state assessments as well. For example, Michigan's first career development assessment included 21,500 students in 1979. Several intriguing findings emerged from these data (Mastie and Handwerger, 1980; Michigan Educational Assessment Program, 1980): More than 60 percent of the Michigan fourth-graders agreed that people should always get paid for working. This leads us to wonder where volunteerism, homemaking, family and community tasks, and other nonpaid endeavors fit into the fourth-grader's work values. Not surprisingly, this mercenary streak continues. Although 80 percent of Michigan tenth-graders indicated that they expected to be working part-time during high school, only 15 percent expected to do volunteer work. Yet, volunteer work is an excellent way for young people to gain experience and explore possible career fields.

The same survey found that sex-role stereotyping was firmly in place by the beginning of fourth grade. Boys and girls indicated significantly different patterns of interests, leisure activities, and preferences. Many of these expectations had been set at home or reflected community values. School practitioners who studied the data concluded that it was far too late to take steps in later elementary and junior high grades to undo the thinking that presently keeps young people out of nontraditional careers.

Only 40 percent of the seventh-graders were able to estimate accurately the time required for the attainment of various goals, a critical step in the acquisition of planning skills. Not only does this finding have important implications for curriculum planners, it helps to explain to subject area teachers and parents why long-range assignments are put off until the last possible moment.

Finally, employability skills were found to be seriously lacking in the Michigan tenth-graders. Although roughly half recognized different sources of occupational information and what they contained, only 5 percent had used at least four common sources. Even using the most generous scoring tolerances, only 60 percent performed adequately in a simulated job interview, only 30 percent filled out a job application form acceptably, and only 5 percent could write an acceptable letter of application. If educators are to respond to the frequent criticism of local employers that high school graduates have no job-seeking skills, data such as these will help both to document the problem and to suggest curricular remedies.

As noted earlier, the performance objectives developed for the national and state assessments can help practitioners to answer the question, Where should my students be in their career development? Clearly, the examples just cited to illustrate the richness of the data being generated by large-scale assessments answer a second question, Where are they? Either the generic data or, if possible, local data using the same assessment materials will provide some important answers for planning.

The assessment projects, which were born of the accountability movement and which grow in number as the push for competence continues, are with us to stay. It is imperative for practitioners to become aware of the resources that these projects offer. Many materials are available free or at cost because they are in the public domain. The new NAEP contractor, Educational Testing Service, has offered to serve as clearinghouse for items and materials from state and national assessments. These items constitute a significant source of assistance to front-line educators in documentating need, targeting curriculum, and evaluating programs.

What Tests Are Available?

"We've been sending tests out to do our dirty work for a long time," observed David P. Campbell, one of the authors of the Strong-Campbell Interest Inventory, before a packed house during the annual convention of the American Personnel and Guidance Association in Washington, D.C., in March 1983. "We need to remember," Campbell continued, "That tests are unpopular when used for the benefit of the institution but popular when used for the benefit of the individual." Much of the negativism associated with testing results from the fact that tests are frequently used to screen people in or out, to justify awkward selection decisions, and to serve institutions rather than individuals. Campbell reminded counselors that people like to take tests. They volunteer to complete tests in popular magazines. He predicted that consumers would be buying individual pocket calculator inventories of interests, personality styles, and so on within the next ten to fifteen years.

In truth, it frequently comes as a surprise to counselors setting up career guidance testing programs that these are so eagerly received by the same students who begrudge other testing interruptions. These tests, the students seem to feel, are for them, not only for the school.

Ask Why. The first essential question that practitioners must ask in setting up career guidance testing programs is why? What will the student get out of the test? What will the staff get out of the test for the counseling program, the career education program, and the vocational education program? These questions have practical answers that guide the instrument selection process.

Instrument selection is never an easy process. Recent developments have exacerbated the difficulty for counselors. The number of published tests and assessment intruments available for vocational guidance and career development program needs has grown enormously in recent years. Familiar interest inventories and aptitude batteries have been supplemented by measures of work values; career development and career maturity instruments; personality, temperament, and style inventories; combined assessment programs; card sorts; and a variety of instruments for special populations. For example, Kapes and Parrish review tools for handicapped persons in Chapter Four.

Busy counselors on the front line need help to assimilate these developments, understand what the new instruments can do, and select tests appropriate for their students. For example, the career maturity instruments represent not simply new tests but an entirely new kind of test that measures the career development process itself — how far the individual student has come in his or her career development process, how complete the student's self-awareness is, how much the student knows about the world of work, how well the student is learning to plan, and so on. Many of the new instruments from the commercial publishers parallel positive features of national and state assessments.

Ask How. Beyond even the various types or categories of instruments now available, counselors face a staggering array of choices. Selection of appropriate instruments must begin with several questions: Who is going to give the test? Who will score it? Who will interpret it? How much time do we have to give it? How long can we wait for results? How much money is available? Once again, the answers to these questions guide the instrument selection process.

Among the many tests now available, practitioners will find some that meet all their requirements in these practical matters. Tests are timed or untimed; secure or "loose"; hand-scorable or machine-scorable; paper-and-pencil or demonstration/manipulation; group-administered or individually administered; computer-administered, self-administered, clerk-administered, or professionally administered; inexpensive or costly; reusable or consumable.

Furthermore, instruments also vary widely in their strength. Some are backed by decades of research, impeccable psychometric qualities, and accurate and helpful counselor support materials, such as manuals, interpretive case studies, profile sheets, and other innovations. Other tests suffer from such difficulties as exaggerated claims of usefulness; sex, race, socioeconomic status, or other bias problems; questionable reliability, validity, or norms; missing research data and technical manuals; or other weaknesses that cause measurement professionals to question their overall reputability. Of course, some excellent new instruments offer attractive features, but they need time to mature. Unfortunately, practitioners often report that they are unable to assess the quality of an instrument; as a result, they defer to the judgments of experts. To counter this trend, Westbrook and Mastie (1983) have suggested a series of practical steps that practitioners can take to evaluate an instrument for a particular purpose; these authors conclude (p. 26): "Make your decision yourself, and make it carefully. Demand excellence. Hold to the expectation that any instrument worth your consideration will meet the rigorous standards of the profession."

Other evidence of the attractiveness of a given instrument that practitioners welcome is data on the level of its use nationwide. Somehow, an instrument feels safer if it is widely used by one's colleagues. In spring 1979, Dale Prediger (1980) and his colleagues at the American College Testing Program undertook a survey of career guidance testing in secondary schools nationwide. That study yielded the list of the top twenty instruments shown in Table 1; in this list, selective use is distinguished from use with most of the students in a grade.

As Table 1 shows, the Armed Services Vocational Aptitude Battery (ASVAB) is the most commonly used test in the country. No group of practitioners shown these data has even failed to recognize the reason instantly: The ASVAB is free. But, they are more than a little uncomfortable with the evidence of its high use, given the frequent analyses of its difficulties in the professional literature.

Table 1. Rank Order of Top Twenty Instruments According to Use

Title	Any use	Use with 30 to 100 percent of the students in a grade
Armed Services Vocational Aptitude Battery (ASVAB)	1	1
General Aptitude Test Battery (GATB)	2	5
Differential Aptitude Test (DAT) (ability measures only)	3	2
Kuder Occupational Interest Survey	4	7
Strong Vocational Interest Blank or Strong-Campbell Interest Inventory	5	8
Kuder Vocational or General Interest Survey	6	6
Ohio Vocational Interest Survey (OVIS)	7	4
Differential Aptitude Test (DAT) (Career Planning Program)	8	3
Self-Directed Search (SDS)	9	9
California Occupational Preference Survey (COPS)	10	12.5
JOB-O	11.5	12.5
Vocational Interest, Experience, and Skills Assessment (VIESA)	11.5	15.5
State career information system	13	10
Local or unpublished instrument	14	12.5
Harrington/O'Shea System for Career Decision Making	16	15.5
Career Planning Program (ACT-CPP)	16	12.5
Career Maturity Inventory (CMI)	16	17
Hall Occupational Orientation Inventory	18	18
IDEAS	19.5	19
Picture Interest Exploration Survey (PIES)	19.5	20

Source: Prediger, 1980, p. 2.

Aside from the ASVAB, the popularity data suggest that the counselors are selecting rather well, although they seem to be sticking with a small number of tried-and-true instruments that have stood the test of time. Both the GATB and the DAT, for example, are decades old and highly respected. It is unfortunate that some very innovative and promising new instruments are not able to dislodge some weaker instruments from their positions on the list. For this to happen, counselors and career education professionals need access to descriptive and evaluative information on the variety of instruments available to them.

The Counselor's Guide. In fall 1982, the National Vocational Guidance Association (NVGA) published *A Counselor's Guide to Vocational Guidance Instruments* (Kapes and Mastie, 1982), which assembles test descriptions and critical evaluations for practitioners who are trying to assess the instruments now available in the rapidly changing field of career guidance measurement. Forty instruments selected by a national advisory panel are described in detail, together with such specifics as target population, purpose, date, time required, types of scores, scale titles, norm groups, costs, scoring options, and a list of all published reviews. Each description is followed by a brief critical review by a national expert. These reviews cite problems that practitioners need to consider in direct, practical terms. Seventy other instruments are listed and annotated without detailed reviews. Other chapters in the *Guide* include a brief review of measurement statistics, a policy statement on appropriate uses, a selected bibliography, and the addresses of publishers of tests cited in the *Guide*. Practitioners should find that the *Guide* allows them to focus on a list of specific tests that should offer a best fit to the local situation.

Another resource book worthy of note is Zunker's *Using Assessment Results in Career Counseling* (1982). This sourcebook of practical case histories shows how test results can be used in counseling with individual clients. Zunker includes a wide variety of types of tests and particular instruments and provides clear illustrations of the score reports and discussions of problems and issues in using them.

Together, these two new resources represent a major advance in the quality and usefulness of reference information on career guidance testing for practitioners. They also meet a number of needs not served by occasional reviews and technical entries in measurement journals and yearbooks. The latter by definition are too old to contain the newest tests, too expensive to be on every counselor's desk, often too statistical for people on the front lines, and too costly to produce and maintain often enough to keep up with new instruments and refinements of value to local practitioners.

How Does Testing Work for the Practitioner?

A few conditions are prerequisite to a happy experience with career guidance testing: First, measuring instruments must be selected to meet specific needs and conditions in the particular local situation. Second, tests must be properly administered and scored. Third, scores must be interpreted accurately and appropriately for the needs of the individual. Fourth, test results must be placed in perspective as just one of the many sources of data that can be related meaningfully to other information. If those conditions are met, the practitioner who has used formal testing in the career guidance program will be pleasantly surprised. In addition to seeing students enjoy testing and await the results eagerly, practitioners may find that a number of other positive outcomes also occur.

Visibility for the Program. Among the earliest benefits of testing is increased visibility. Counselors become actively involved with teachers and classes during test administration. They initiate a relationship with each student tested and acquire a role of perceived facilitator, even if all interpretation must be done in group settings on the first round. In many cases, particularly where some of the new "loose" instruments that can be taken home are used, communication with the home can improve dramatically. And, as a final aspect of visibility, testing serves to differentiate counselors in students' minds from others from whom they may seek career assistance—including peers, family, and friends—by offering a valued service unavailable elsewhere. Since public relations must always be attended to by counseling and career education programs, this payoff in visibility, while it is not the most important outcome, should not be slighted.

Organization, Efficiency, and Structure. While little is learned from testing that could not eventually be unearthed in one-on-one counseling interviews, the group administration and interpretation sessions are vastly more efficient for the first stages of this learning process. Thus, any subsequent individual counseling can move farther and faster. In addition, the results of the exploration process can be related directly to the organization of the data bases and other resources that are available to students in the particular setting. Harris-Bowlsbey examines resources of this nature in Chapter Five.

Cognitive Progress in Students' Career Development. As already noted, tests are probably least important for their ability to generate brand new information for the students. Generally, students respond to the reports of career guidance tests with recognition and clarification. However, the tests do have certain benefits: They get all the self-knowledge out in the open where it is recognized; they share the information with counselors and other facilitators, such as teachers and parents as appropriate; and, perhaps most important, they provide a structure for pulling together the students' present understandings into emerging patterns.

Affective Progress in Students' Career Development. Far more significant than the informational progress may be the affective progress in career development that use of these measuring instruments can foster. The student who recognizes that his or her prior self-knowledge was on target gains in confidence and in readiness to proceed with planning. Overwhelmed students are reassured that there is a place to start and a logical way to proceed. Procrastinating, uninvolved students are offered a reasonably pleasant diversion that gets them off dead center; it can be particularly effective if the counseling center has access to one of the new computerized versions. Students whose present planning and self-knowledge need to be stretched, modified, or made more realistic are offered "safe" boundaries within which to work. (However, it should be noted that computer-generated narrative reports appear to be very threatening to a student when the student's own thinking is different from the test data. Information can acquire the aura of truth when the computer is speaking. Harris-Bowlsbey considers this issue in Chapter Five.) Other affective benefits can be seen in the ease with which testing can facilitate movement to action steps by offering an informational base and the security of a system or process. Finally, tests of this nature refuse to yield unidirectional one-right-job answers. This encourages exploration, flexibility, comfort with present alternatives and future changes, and belief in many appropriate choices and career paths.

Program Management. For situations in which the instrument used is either one of the new commercially published career development or career maturity tests or one of the instruments available through the large-scale assessment programs, a number of other benefits speak to program management. Such instruments can demonstrate needs, convince funding agencies or administrators of program urgency, target program interventions for maximum value, monitor progress in the provision of services, and offer a means for evaluating the program through pre- and post data. For most practitioners, these program management–related outcomes are the least convincing reasons for adding testing to the career counseling program. However, their importance in some situations cannot be denied.

What Lies Ahead?

Of the significant changes that career guidance practitioners will encounter in the decade ahead, a number of the most profound are addressed elsewhere in this volume. It is imperative for counselors to hear the challenges conveyed in the discussions of changing job futures, new technologies, and increasing responsibilities for special populations. They must then consider the implications of each issue for their own local testing program.

At the same time, a few additional reflections on the future of career guidance testing are in order here. For example, some excellent instruments may disappear for lack of use. Already, the Assessment of Career Development has been withdrawn, and a small number of others may be in jeopardy. Resources like Kapes and Mastie (1982) help, since people are desperate for assistance with selection. But, we cannot expect commercial publishers to wait forever to be discovered. There will be continuous revision, updating, and strengthening of a few of the strongest instruments, such as the Differential Aptitude Tests (DAT, Forms V and W), the Ohio Vocational Interest Survey (OVIS II), and measures in computer-assisted guidance systems such as DISCOVER.

Even the military sponsors of the Armed Services Vocational Aptitude Battery are now accepting extensive help from the profession. An increasing number of combined assessment packages will appear. Many will offer multidimensional measurement at one time for efficiency and comparable data.

Test results will be increasingly tied to large data bases to facilitate exploration as a next step. Sex restrictiveness will be closely monitored. The separate sex norms that are imperative now on some instruments will perhaps yield to a changing population. Recalibration of test results to newer occupational titles will continue as the work force changes rapidly. It is possible that some entirely new trait or component will begin to be measured if it appears that an identifiable new aptitude, interest, or value is needed for the eighties.

Creative financing will address the problem of costs of testing. Site scoring will increase, as will regional sharing of test supplies. Block grants and similar funding sources will be used. Similar techniques will be sought and found. Redundant testing will be replaced by multiple uses of test data. Wider variation in test plans in a given setting will accommodate the needs of more individuals, including special populations, with fewer all-group administrations. Computer-adaptive testing will be invaluable in certain settings. However, because of hardware costs and the large numbers to be served, computer testing may never replace paper-and-pencil testing in the schools. Finally, consumer attitudes toward career guidance testing will continue to be positive, and uses will extend to assisting with leisure choices and retirement options.

The inescapable picture is one of practitioners' continuing need to update their knowledge and skills. Because of the unique contributions that career guidance testing can make to a program and to individuals it is here to stay. Changes will also continue. It is imperative for vehicles like this volume to continue to be produced and disseminated to the field in a massive ongoing in-service attempt. This is no small challenge.

References

Aubrey, R. F. *Career Development Needs of Thirteen-Year-Olds.* Arlington, Va.: National Vocational Guidance Association and Association for Measurement in Guidance, 1978.

Campbell, D. P. "A Strong-Campbell Interest Inventory Update: New Developments, New Interpretation." Presentation at the annual meeting of the American Personnel and Guidance Association, March 1983, Washington, D.C.

Educational Testing Service. *Iowa Career Education Inventory.* Des Moines: Iowa Department of Public Instruction, 1981.

Jepsen, D. A. "Test Usage in the 1970s: A Summary and Interpretation." *Measurement and Evaluation in Guidance,* 1982, *15* (2), 164–168.

Kapes, J. T., and Mastie, M. M. *A Counselor's Guide to Vocational Guidance Instruments.* Alexandria, Va.: National Vocational Guidance Association, 1982.

Martin, W. H. "National Assessment of Educational Progress." In J. E. Milholland (Ed.), *Insights from Large-Scale Surveys.* New Directions for Testing and Measurement, no. 2. San Francisco: Jossey-Bass, 1979.

Mastie, M. M., and Handwerger, K. H. "Career Development Skills: Do You Know if Your Students Have Them?" *AREA Newsletter,* 1980, *13* (1), 7.

Michigan Educational Assessment Program. *Career Development Assessment Series: Statewide Results, Grades 4, 7, and 10.* Lansing: Michigan Educational Assessment Program, Michigan State Board of Education, 1980.

Michigan Educational Assessment Program. *Essential Performance Objectives for Career Development.* Lansing: Michigan Educational Assessment Program, Michigan State Board of Education, 1983.

Miller, J. V. *Career Development Needs of Nine-Year-Olds.* Arlington, Va.: National Vocational Guidance Association and Association for Measurement and Evaluation in Guidance, 1978.

Miller, J. V. "1970s Trends in Assessing Career Counseling, Guidance, and Education." *Measurement and Evaluation in Guidance,* 1982, *15* (2), 142–145.

Mitchell, A. M. *Career Development Needs of Seventeen-Year-Olds.* Arlington, Va.: National Vocational Guidance Association and Association for Measurement and Evaluation in Guidance, 1978.

National Assessment of Educational Progress. *Objectives for Career and Occupational Development.* Denver: National Assessment of Educational Progress, 1971.

National Assessment of Educational Progress. *Objectives for Career and Occupational Development: Second Assessment.* Denver: National Assessment of Educational Progress, 1977.

Prediger, D. J. *ACT's Nationwide Survey of Career Guidance Testing.* Iowa City: American College Testing Program, 1980. Unpublished memorandum to the National Vocational Guidance Association Commission on Assessment and Testing, April 4, 1980.

Rodgers, R. C. *Iowa Career Education Inventory Interpretative Guide and Technical Report.* Evanston, Ill.: Educational Testing Service, 1983.

Tiedeman, D. B., and others. *The Cross Sectional Story of Early Career Development as Revealed by the National Assessment of Educational Progress.* Arlington, Va.: National Vocational Guidance Association and Association for Measurement and Evaluation in Guidance, 1978.

Westbrook, B. W. *Career Development Needs of Adults.* Arlington, Va.: National Vocational Guidance Association and Association for Measurement and Evaluation in Guidance, 1978.

Westbrook, B. W., and Mastie, M. M. "Doing Your Homework: Suggestions for the Evaluation of Tests by Practitioners." *Educational Measurement: Issues and Practices,* 1983, *2* (1), 11–14, 26.

Zunker, V. G. *Using Assessment Results in Career Counseling.* Monterey, Calif.: Brooks/Cole, 1982.

Marjorie M. Mastie is a measurement and guidance consultant for the Washtenaw Intermediate School District in Ann Arbor, Michigan. She has guided career development assessment programs for the National Assessment of Educational Progress and the Michigan Educational Assessment Program.

Since the pioneering study by Thorndike and Hagen (1959) almost twenty-five years ago, technology and a host of political and economic forces have widened the gulf between what the individual job seeker wants to know and what current sources of occupational information can deliver.

Coping with Occupational Information Overload

Frank H. Cassell
Ronald C. Rodgers

Occupational choice has long been recognized as an integral part of adult life, requiring trade-offs between the advantages and disadvantages of various types of work. Adam Smith ([1776], 1964) described the elements of choice in terms of the concept of net advantage. He identified five elements of choice. Each helps to define the occupational information of interest to the person who examines the job and to the employer who considers applicants. These five factors are: the agreeableness of the work; the difficulty and expense of learning the skills required: the security of employment in the job; the status and prestige of those who perform the job successfully; and the probability of success, failure, and future opportunities.

These elements have been discussed and refined by many analysts and researchers. Parsons (1909, p. 5) defined a wise choice of vocation as one that balanced a person's "aptitudes, abilities, interests, ambitions, resources, and limitations" with "knowledge of the requirements and conditions of success, advantages and disadvantages, compensation, opportunities, and prospects in different lines of work." Freud ([1930], 1961, p. 27) considered work "a source of special satisfaction if it is freely chosen," although he was quick to add that "the great majority of people work only under the stress of necessity." Menninger (1942, p. 138) ranked work first "of all methods for absorbing the aggres-

R. C. Rodgers (Ed.). *Measurement Trends in Career and Vocational Education.* New Directions for Testing and Measurement, no. 20. San Francisco: Jossey-Bass, December 1983.

sive energies of mankind in a useful direction" and concluded (p. 158) that "perhaps next to the choice of a marital partner [vocation] is the most important and far-reaching decision made by the individual." Hall (1921), Ginzberg and others (1951), Super (1957), Erikson (1963), Havighurst (1972), Ginzberg (1972), and Wirtz (1975) are among those who have emphasized the importance of work and occupational choice for youth and adults.

Ginzberg (1972, p. 170) synthesized much of this thinking and research into a definition of occupational choice that integrates Smith's concept of net advantage with Parsons' view of occupational information and decision making: "Occupational choice is a lifelong process of decision making in which the individual seeks to find the optimal fit between his career preparation and goals and the realities of the world of work." Ginzberg amplifies this modern view (p. 172) by urging flexibility as "men and women seek the best occupational fit between their changing desires and their changing circumstances.... The principal challenge that young people face during their teens is to develop a strategy that will keep their options open."

Transitions and Recurrent Choices

Every labor market includes large numbers of people who are in transition from one occupational decision to another: from school to work, from part-time work to full-time work, from unemployment to a job, from one job to another, and so on. Recent data from the Bureau of Labor Statistics (BLS) (Bureau of Labor Statistics, 1982) indicate that one of every five persons who left any job in 1980 changed occupations. It is still more startling that the BLS estimate excludes people, such as high school or college graduates making the transition from full-time student to work, who entered or returned to the labor market without having held a job earlier that year.

Two types of transitions are of special importance: those of young people making initial occupational choices and those of unemployed adults. Both groups want and need detailed occupational information, but information must be interpreted and presented differently due to the individual needs, interests, experience, and preferences of these groups.

Helping Youth to Prepare for Better Jobs. The entry-level worker faces more than the need to select a first job. Rodgers (1975, 1976) cites numerous studies that find teenagers benefiting from part-time or temporary jobs while still in high school. However, most of these jobs are in the secondary labor market, where few specific skills and limited training are required. Such jobs typically provide casual supervision and working conditions, low pay, few benefits, and little encouragement to develop work habits needed to move into better jobs (Doeringer and Piore, 1971). Fast-food, discount retailing, and entertainment industries all depend on such teenage or low-cost help. While these jobs provide income and while they can be instructive to the person who uses them to learn firsthand about the differences between good and bad jobs, many youth are unable to tell the difference.

The good jobs typically exist in the primary labor market, where many of the skills, experiences, and other resources needed to adapt to more demanding opportunities in an organization are learned on the job (Doeringer and Piore, 1971). Such on-the-job training is sometimes available in secondary labor market jobs, but only for the young worker who brings these expectations to a job or who happens to become an apprentice to a supervisor or mentor with that view. Opportunities to learn what is needed for advancement are rarely designed into secondary labor market jobs.

Trow (1979, p. 138) reaches a similar conclusion, urging that youth policies focus on "the transition from the secondary to the primary labor market." Rodgers (1976, p. 24) adds: "Continuous referral to secondary market jobs, where opportunity for growth and development is often limited if not foreclosed, may trap a person in low-skilled, low-paying jobs for life." These are jobs where "workers with employment disadvantages tend to work" (Doeringer and Piore, 1971, p. 166). Doeringer and Piore continue (p. 167): "It may be quite appropriate for workers for whom the job itself is a secondary aspect of their lives, whose income requirements are limited (as in the case of teenagers without families), or who foresee eventual access to primary employment. It is the permanent and involuntary confinement in the secondary market of workers with major family responsibilities that poses the problem."

Assisting Adults with the Stress of Unemployment. The frustration of occupational choice is no longer focused solely on youth. The days when a person could count on making a single lifetime commitment to one occupation appear to be gone forever. Mastie supports that view in Chapter One, as do Hecker (1983) and recent BLS data (Bureau of Labor Statistics, 1982). Perhaps nowhere is this experience more stressful than when its cause is sudden, involuntary unemployment.

Brenner (1976) documented significant national patterns linking high unemployment with suicide rates, rising criminal violence, and declining mental and physical health. Involuntary job loss appears to trigger a process similar to that caused by the sudden loss of a loved one to death (Kubler-Ross, 1969). Swinburne (1981) suggests that this process involves a pattern of shock, optimism, pessimism, fatalism, and adjustment. Amundson and Borgen (1982) emphasize the need to help the victim of such stress to retain the identity of unemployed *worker* to avoid the frustration and apathy that accompany the identity of unemployed *person.*

Parson and others (1983) suggest that there are three stages, each with parallels to the grieving process: job loss, accompanied by denial, anger, and bargaining; initial job search, characterized by optimism and acceptance of the situation if the person can resume working in a short time; otherwise, this is likely to be followed by prolonged job search, burnout, frustration, pessimism, deteriorating self-confidence, and apathy. Once an otherwise capable adult with many years of successful job performance enters the third stage, that individual requires much more than information about jobs. Such a person must first regain the confidence to consider opportunities in light of his or her capabilities, experience, interests, and preferences. Information or encouragement alone is seldom enough to restore the confidence required to meet the challenge of an unfamiliar occupation, training program, industry, or organization.

Newly unemployed adults surveyed by Parson and others (1983) had a clear, rational view of their needs for occupational information. They rated as most important information about reemployment (looking for work, job placement, recovering medical benefits, job retraining) and coping with the critical financial burdens of sudden unemployment (food, family budgets, saving money, housing, energy conservation, and staying healthy). They also preferred to rely on personal contacts and workshops for the information about reemployment and on pamphlets and other mass-produced or media sources for the survival information.

The long-term unemployed are likely to encounter far more problems, especially during the next few years. Resources to assist the chronically unemployed are shrinking rapidly. A person who exhausts or who never qualified for unemployment insurance benefits is not counted in BLS measures of the unemployed. The Comprehensive Employment and Training Act (CETA) of 1973 supported services to youth and adults who had little experience and few skills — that is, who had little chance of moving quickly into secure, primary labor market jobs with a nominal amount of training and job placement assistance. However, performance standards in the new Job Training Partnership Act (JPTA) of 1982, which replaced CETA on October 1, 1983, are likely to shift attention toward the most skilled persons among the unemployed. Large numbers of those less likely to succeed will be referred to welfare, other programs, or back to the unemployed labor force. And, even if the performance standards in JTPA do not create such a climate, rapidly declining federal allocations for service to the unemployed or for training to enable persons to acquire new skills create new pressures to screen out the less skilled applicants for such assistance. Another complication lingering on the horizon is the conflict between workfare as a substitute for welfare and the decline in resources to help the long-term unemployed move from the secondary to the primary labor market. Such barriers may be by-products of popular attitudes that Mastie cited in Chapter One.

Differentiating Between Labor Markets and Local Job Markets

There are many ways of considering occupational information and its role in helping a person to make a wise choice of a vocation. One approach is to define the many labor markets in which these decisions are made not in broad economic terms but in terms of the teenager, adult, and counselor. Classical economic theory tends to treat the labor market as a single abstract entity with fixed features that interact rationally with other elements of the economy. However, both the counselor and the job seeker depend on a more practical view of the local job market in which the job seeker lives and wants to work. Each local market consists of a mix of industries, jobs, employers, and workers "bonded together largely by geography and their collective dependence on other factors in a local, regional, state, or national economy" (Settles, 1982, pp. 1–2).

Thus, the view that one takes of an abstract labor market or of a network of plural job markets in specific industries and locations affects how a person defines relevant information and its value in making occupational choices. Human capital theory examines the role of these factors as people prepare for work. Schultz (1971), an early proponent of this position, identified five categories of investment in human capital: schooling and higher education, on-the-job training, migration, health, and economic information. Schooling and higher education, on-the-job training, and health are reflected in the skills, dependability, and productivity that workers bring to employers in a local job market. Migration and economic information are related to the interaction among local, regional, state, and national job markets.

This chapter builds on human capital theory with a labor market model that focuses on the operational dynamics of five structural elements (Cassell and Rodgers, 1983): labor market demand—the number of jobs classified by location, qualifications, and conditions of employment; labor market supply—the number of persons seeking or interested in work classified by skills, experience, location, and preferred conditions of employment; price—the wages, benefits, incentives, and costs of various jobs commonly referred to in the classical literature as *net advantage*; labor market intermediaries—persons and institutions that offer training, job placement, testing, guidance, job survival skills, and related supportive services; and labor market information—knowledge that can enable job seekers and employers to make more efficient and accurate choices.

The labor market is the marketplace where workers and employers exchange services and benefits and where workers make transitions from one occupation or job to another. Supply and demand change constantly in response to economic and social conditions, personal values, and rising levels of education. Workers provide skills, knowledge, time, and services. Employers provide wages and benefits, economic security, and the conditions and incentives that attract and hold good workers. Price serves as a proxy for net advantage in its role as the initial allocator of labor and jobs. The process is aided by information that enables workers and employers to compare and select jobs and applicants. Intermediaries improve the quality of such decisions by interpreting information so that workers and employers can make better, more efficient choices about a wider range of opportunities.

The traditional definition of labor supply is the number of persons available for and actively seeking or engaged in work. However, this definition often ignores the discouraged workers who are ineligible for or who have exhausted unemployment insurance benefits. Such persons can lose faith and interest in systematic job search efforts if despair, apathy, and pessimism convince them that there is little chance of finding a decent job. Other persons enter and leave the labor supply voluntarily in order to attend school, bear or raise children, increase leisure time, or invest their energies in unpaid work at home or in community service. These choices are especially frequent among those in the secondary labor market, where work provides insufficient rewards to be the most important part of their life.

Labor demand includes both current and anticipated employment by skill level, occupation, industry, and location. Demand is influenced by the condition of national, regional, state, and local economies. To justify the need for a new employee, an employer must forecast whether the productivity that the new worker adds can be recovered with new income for the organization.

Price reflects the net advantage of wages, benefits, costs, and incentives associated with each type of employment. Traditional labor market theory assumes that price is a sufficient mediating force between labor supply and demand. Human capital theory attempts to account for imperfect information and flaws in how workers and employers learn about each other.

This view of net advantage is dynamic and complex. It requires the job seeker to evaluate the conditions and characteristics of a job, then to arrive at decisions based on trade-offs between what the job seeker desires and what the job offers. Cassell and Cassell (1981) extend this analysis of net advantage to include strategies for analyzing internal labor markets, which consist of job and career choices within particular organizations. Campbell considers these work adjustment issues in Chapter Three.

The employer also varies price as part of a net advantage decision. The more critical and difficult it is to acquire a certain set of skills in a worker, the more attractive the employer tries to make the wages, benefits, and conditions of the job. As the demand for particular skills critical to more than one industry increases, the cost of finding and keeping good workers with those skills also rises. As the competition for other skills declines, the wages and benefits required to attract and keep these workers can level off or decrease.

Labor market information is a key ingredient in assessing net advantage as workers and employers compare opportunities in local markets. The person needs to know who is hiring for which jobs; where and when; the working conditions and performance requirements for each job; and the future risks and advancement opportunities. Employers need to know when and where people with the skills that they require are available for work; they also need predictive information about each applicant's probable behavior and productivity in a particular job.

There is an intriguing conflict between what is needed and what is available. The best data documenting labor supply are at the local level, while the best information about labor demand is in the national data. Thus, the quality of the information is seriously flawed at both ends of the matching process. BLS forecasts of occupational outlook match excellent estimates of demand with weak measures of labor supply (Rugg, 1983), while local efforts to match individuals with specific jobs occur with reasonably good information about labor supply but with weak information about local demand (Rodgers, 1977; Rodgers and Cassell, 1976, 1977). Local demand data in state career information systems and their commercial counterparts do not address this problem adequately (Stevens, 1976). Despite nearly eight years of additional effort, Stevens' (1976) label of this problem as "mission impossible" still appears to be appropriate. Both national information about labor supply and local information about labor demand are fragmented, often out of date by the time they are estimated, and difficult and costly to acquire.

Labor market intermediaries try to resolve some of these imperfections in the market by interpreting the complex assessments of risks, benefits, conditions, and costs for workers and employers. The goal of these intermediaries is to increase the efficiency of the matching process. If they succeed, both the employer and the worker benefit from savings in the cost and time of the job search. If the worker has been receiving unemployment insurance benefits, the intermediary can also lower costs to all employers in a state by reducing unemployment insurance costs. Cassell and Rodgers (1978) offer a detailed examination of this issue in an assessment of the role of the U.S. Employment Service as a labor market intermediary. Intermediaries perform their roles by sharing information about price, labor supply, and demand in local, state, and national job markets. Employers want lists of qualified applicants, while the job seeker wants a list of job openings matched with his or her skills, experience, interests, and preferences.

Who are the intermediaries? Nearly everyone is or can become a labor market intermediary. Rodgers (1977) divides the intermediaries into two groups. Formal intermediaries include teachers, counselors, personnel workers, and others who intend to help people to prepare for and adapt to the requirements of work. Informal intermediaries include parents, friends, supervisors, co-workers, and others who help a person to learn about jobs and their requirements. Many of the informal intermediaries exert subtle or unintentional influences, but their impact is often far greater than that of the formal intermediaries. This is especially true of those who help to shape basic attitudes about learning, work, self-confidence, perceptions of personal strengths and limitations, and capacity to adapt to new demands and opportunities. Schooling can also help young people to develop habits of work discipline, adaptation to supervision, and perseverance.

Sources and Limitations of Occupational Classification and Information Systems

Rugg (1983) cautions counselors about the conflicts and limitations noted earlier with an insightful analysis of inconsistencies and assumptions that can undermine projections of occupational outlook. The Committee on Occupational Analysis of the National Research Council offers an even more severe critique of the *Dictionary of Occupational Titles* (DOT) and of related classification and information resources (Miller and others, 1980). Both these analyses demonstrate the size of the gulf between what the job seeker and the employer want to know about each other and the ability of current information resources to meet their needs.

Despite their limitations, such resources as the DOT and the Occupational Employment Statistics (OES) program, both products of the U.S. Department of Labor, are extremely valuable. If their limitations are recognized and if these resources are properly used, they can be extremely helpful to counselors and clients. However, there are signs that counselors often credit these sources with more precision than may be appropriate for the individual job seeker in the local job market. The American Psychological Association (1974, p. 31) asserts that "no test is valid for all purposes or in all situations or for all groups of individuals." *Perhaps it is time to apply a similar standard to the validity of various uses of each type and source of occupational information.* Miller and others (1980) raise this issue in their critique of the DOT. They ask a long list of questions that can undermine many of the assumptions that users of existing national data sources appear to make when they apply projections and classifications to individual job seekers and employers in local job markets.

The issue is that too little sensitivity may have been shown to the use of such information: How can it be used without exceeding the limitations under which it has been assembled and reported? While the BLS publications are typically the best available, progress in helping the individual job seeker and employer to make personal sense of such information may depend on careful attention to the limitations. There is no reason to stop using the DOT and other available data bases, but there is an urgent need for greater caution in matching national trends with individual job seekers, counselors, and employers. The paragraphs that follow synthesize many of these concerns and their impact on the counselor, the job seeker, and the employer.

Shifting Occupational and Employment Demand. Efforts have been made at the BLS and elsewhere to respond to these criticisms, but much more needs to be done. Carey (1981, p. 3) begins a discussion of a three-scenario approach—best, middle, and worst assumptions—used by the BLS in its occupational outlook projections for 1982–1983 by noting that "economic projections can be no more accurate than the assumptions that underlie them." Rugg (1983, p. 347) expands on this point: "Because the essence of any projection methodology is a systematic extension of past trends into the future, unexpected and never before experienced changes in the national economy are major obstacles to the accuracy of occupational outlook projections." Changes in government spending, international energy supplies, trade imbalances, and countless other political and economic factors can trigger never before experienced changes that alter the demand for workers in various occupations, locations, and industries. Each new shift can undermine the assumptions on which projections have been based.

Unrealistic Assumptions. Rugg (1983, p. 347) argues that the BLS projections may also be unrealistically optimistic, even with the three-scenario approach: "The current BLS projections to 1990 were based on the assumptions that inflation will decelerate to 5.2 percent annually by 1990, that unemployment will fall to 4.5 percent by the mid 1980s and remain stable thereafter, and that energy prices will increase only 3 percent per year. Obviously, the use of such optimistic estimates of key economic variables is likely to inflate projections of economic growth as well as employment."

As of this writing, unemployment has little chance of falling below eight percent in most major economic forecasts through 1985. This difference alone could mean that several million more individuals will suffer the consequences of unemployment each year. In addition, Hecker (1983) reports that only recently have BLS projections included job openings resulting from projected replacement needs identified by the Current Population Survey (CPS), which is conducted monthly as part of the employment statistics program. Yet, several more times the number of jobs available from even the best-case projections of economic growth occur due to replacement needs: "An astonishing 23.2 million openings annually, on average, are projected for the 1980s, based on the low trend scenario. There were actually more than 20 million in 1980, when 21.5 million people" found new jobs (Hecker, 1983, p. 27).

Obsolete Policy Targets. The implications of major shifts in federal or state policy are seldom known immediately. However, each set of outlook projections must assume stable policy targets, although these policy targets can change radically in a very short period of time. Rugg (1983, p. 347) illustrates the problem: "The current projections for 1990 that were published in 1980 were formulated during the Carter Administration using policy targets that were in effect at that time. Economic policy has changed dramatically since then under the Reagan administration, but such changes will not be reflected in occupational outlook projections until 1982, when new 1990 projections are released by the BLS." The BLS *Occupational Projections and Training Data, 1982 Edition* (Bureau of Labor Statistics, 1982) is silent on how such policy shifts have altered assumptions or results of the new outlook projections.

Inadequate Data to Support Users' Assumptions. Miller and others (1980) report many examples of job analysis information in the DOT that are ten to twenty-five years old or that are based on inadequate numbers of employers within the particular industry to offer valid information. Although individual job requirements within an organization appear to change very slowly (Cassell and others, 1975), there is no reason to assume that such data remain valid indefinitely. Carey (1980) also found that occupational staffing patterns within industries varied far more than the distributions forecast from the industry-occupation matrix methods used in BLS data. The Occupational Employment Statistics (OES) program tries to respond to this issue, but the 1980 projections were the first to include OES data for industrial staffing patterns (Pilot, 1980). Finally, Miller and others (1980) make twenty-two recommendations for improving the DOT and conclude (p. 16) by urging that "the next edition of the DOT should not be issued until substantial improvements in the occupational analysis program have been made."

Weak Supply-Side Data. As noted earlier, another major limitation of the national data is information about the competition for various jobs. This is especially true of secondary labor market jobs, which typically do not require specialized education or skills. Hecker (1983, p. 27) reports that nine of the ten occupations with the greatest numbers of projected annual openings in the 1980s do not require a degree for entry, and half "can usually be entered without any special training or experience at all. Most people who enter these occupations are young, and many work part-time. Eight are predominantly held by women. Many people take these jobs to earn money for school or to supplement family income while tending to household responsibilities and do not stay in them very long. A large proportion of people in these jobs transfer" to other occupations. This is a classic description of the kind of high-turnover unattractive job that anyone who wants to make a serious career commitment will shun. However, in poorer economic times, people with skills will compete for such jobs until they can find better opportunities. In better economic conditions, the disadvantaged and youth dominate such secondary labor market jobs.

Insensitivity to Local Economic Climates. The last limitation to be cited here may be the most severe for the counselor and the individual job seeker. Even if all the improvements called for by the studies and analyses just cited were completed today, counselors and other labor market intermediaries would still have to help interpret information for the individual job seeker. For most youth and adults in search of jobs, the issue is not one of how many thousand openings exist nationally but of how they can qualify for the particular opportunities available locally. Turner (1980) analyzes the U.S. Employment Service's Automated Matching System as one response to this problem. However, many good jobs are never listed with the Employment Service, and both workers and employers in many urban markets consider that system the intermediary of last resort. Cassell and Rodgers (1978) examine the role and problems of the federal employment service system in detail.

State projections based on manipulation of national data sources often smooth out or ignore local and state variations and market conditions — precisely the level where most counselors and their clients want and need good information. As a result, best-case estimates can create an illusion of precision that is not justified by the limitations and assumptions that underlie the data. Unfortunately, the local or state data provided in many computer-assisted occupational information and guidance systems are often based on such estimates. Counselors must be cautious in attributing too much value to national and state projections and in interpreting their impact for individual job seekers or employers in local job markets.

Looking to the Future

For the reasons just outlined, it appears that there is a wide gulf between what job seekers, employers, and counselors need and what national projections and their spin-offs can deliver. How can this situation be remedied? Many partial solutions have been suggested, but all depend on selection of a particular occupational classification scheme — or worse, on creation of still another occupational classification scheme. However, what is needed is a system that links information about the individual job seeker with as many existing information and classification resources as possible.

The survey of newly employed workers by Parson and others (1983) offers clues to an approach to this question. These authors found that their clients were extremely sensitive to their need to find a new job as quickly as possible. Unemployed adults preferred to rely on personal contact, workshops, and formal instruction only in areas focused on finding employment or on increasing skills to become more employable, including looking for work, job retraining, résumé preparation, interviewing skills, and higher education. They preferred lower-cost mass-produced or media sources for other information, which they felt was extremely important, but which they also felt they could gather and digest themselves. Martin (1980) offers an excellent resource responsive to these findings with a job hunter's guide to use of the library and other-cost sources of information.

The challenge ahead is to devise new strategies and instruments that link information about the job seeker's skills, experience, interests, and preferences with employment requirements and training opportunities in specific industries and specific employers in local job markets. Many existing resources address individual elements. Many are reviewed briefly by Kapes and Parrish in Chapter Four of this volume, and they have been surveyed in detail by Kapes and Mastie (1982). However, there is still substantial room for improvement in matching information about individual job seekers with individual employers' needs. Such approaches need to synthesize information about local employer and industry requirements with information about local job seekers.

Information About Local Employers' Requirements. As noted earlier, national data have extraordinary value for policy-level decisions but relatively little for the individual job seeker unless they can be translated into local job-market terms. Strategies to fill this gap in local labor market data have been in use in some locations for many years. Cassell and Rodgers (1976) documented one example in the Baltimore CETA program. Rodgers (1976) refined a low-cost local labor market survey methodology in an essentially rural region; Rodgers and Cassell (1976, 1977) extended this into local models that even small CETA staffs could carry out. Each strategy supplements national data sources with information from local employers. The results can be surprising as local staff discover modules of employment opportunities among employers that they might have overlooked if they had not gathered local job market data.

Current provisions of the new Job Training Partnership Act (JTPA) should make such assessments even more necessary and accessible today. The new legislation empowers employers who serve on local Private Industry Councils (PICs) to specify training programs and standards for judging when JTPA clients are job-ready. One key element in any system that matches local workers with local jobs must be clear specifications of the knowledge, skills, and abilities essential to local employment and training opportunities. The best source of such information should be the employers in each local market.

When detailed local data do not meet this need, national sources, such as the DOT, census codes classifying occupations (SOCs) and industries (SICs), and such U.S. Employment Service resources as the *Guide to Occupational Exploration* (GOE) can serve as temporary proxies for local specifications. The GOE codes describe sixty-six work groups arranged in twelve interest areas in a format that looks especially promising as a framework for enabling JTPA counselors and their clients to link employer information with local training and worker characteristics. However, the best information is derived directly from employer specifications in local job listings.

The U.S. Employment Service's 2,500 offices and network of state-administered job banks have the potential to meet this need. Unfortunately, there are two major barriers to immediate use of this resource. First, the job bank currently exists on several types of state computer systems, which are not linked with common programming; linking them would require software adjustments to each system and other adaptations (Turner, 1980). Second, state boundaries can place artificial barriers between workers and jobs, especially in major urban areas, such as St. Louis, Cincinnati, Baltimore, Louisville, El Paso, Toledo, Memphis, Hartford, the two Kansas Cities, and the two Portlands (in Oregon and Maine). Some local job markets even may attract workers from three states; these markets include Philadelphia, Mobile, Chicago, New York City, Las Vegas, Boston, Providence, and Washington, D.C. All these operate as local or regional job markets recognized by the Census Bureau as multistate Standardized Metropolitan Statistical Areas (SMSAs), but each area is divided by state boundaries, which can lead job bank systems to operate on different assumptions and to be delivered on separate computer systems.

Thus, one critical element in integrating employer listings and job requirements across state boundaries may call for a national solution that addresses one of the most serious problems targeted by Miller and others (1980): Occupational analysis of job requirements and working conditions data derived from aggregation of employer listings of job requirements and working conditions in a national network of integrated job banks would provide much more secure support for both national and local market information needs.

An interim solution to this problem may be to cross-reference DOT, GOE, SIC, and SOC codes in a single linking network so that local job market information classified by any of these criteria can be interpreted for individual job seekers. This solution also would permit matching the variety of local information resources in a common reporting format as long as they included one of the major DOT, census, or Employment Service coding structures. One resource that goes a long way toward making this feasible is the National Crosswalk Service Center managed by the Iowa State Occupational Information Coordinating Committee with support from the National Occupational Information Coordinating Committee. The service center was created to help state committees link their data and delivery systems with the DOT, census, GOE, and related information and classification systems. Greater use of the resources of the crosswalk service center should improve the local relevance of information for job seekers in programs that rely on any of the major information and classification systems included in this resource.

While use of existing coding systems in the DOT is still not perfect, it can add to a job seeker's knowledge of physical demands, working conditions, skills, training, and other requirements typical of occupations available in local job markets. Information from local employers is always needed to validate national data in terms of local job market requirements, especially in light of the limitations in the DOT occupational analysis program cited by Miller and others (1980). Local data to complement national sources should be well within reach of most JTPA staffs if employers who serve on local PICs are used effectively.

Information About Individual Job Seekers. The next major question in performing the worker-job matching process is to gather sufficient information from and about job seekers so that their skills, interests, experience, and preferences can be reflected in the selection of information most likely to be helpful in identifying local employment and training opportunities appropriate for them. This process, too, is a best-match situation, not a perfect fit. As Mastie comments in Chapter One, there is really no single lifetime right answer in selecting and preparing for employment. Most workers under the age of forty today will make from five to nine occupational transitions.

There are many possible solutions to the questions that need to be asked of the individual job seeker before such matching can occur effectively. Dunn (1983) reports that state-sponsored career information delivery systems already serve thirty-nine states and Washington, D.C. Most of these systems begin with a short self-report in which the computer asks questions to help sort and report occupational information matched with the job seeker's interests. Many private systems also exist. Some either are part of state systems or fill gaps in states that have not elected to sponsor centralized networks. Harris-Bowlsbey examines the impact of such systems in Chapter Five. However, most of these systems lack the capacity to link job-related information about the professional, technical, adaptation, and social skills that individual job seekers have or need to acquire with employer requirements in local jobs. The Educational Testing Service (ETS) and the Radio Corporation of America collaborated in an effort to meet part of this need for the Army's Basic Skills Education Program by producing a series of short training readiness tests designed to recommend appropriate remediation for enlistees interested in programs for which they may lack essential skills ("ETS to Develop Skill Test Battery for Army," 1982). So far, no parallel assessment strategies are available in the civilian labor market.

Cassell and Rodgers (1976) proposed that readiness measures should distinguish among three levels of readiness as a person moves toward successful adaptation to the requirements of a particular industry, employer, and job: *Training readiness* refers to basic skills in reading, computation, the ability to comprehend and follow directions, and other training-specific prerequisites and performance requirements; attitudes toward training; and attitudes toward the industry or occupation related to the training. *Job readiness* refers to entry-level performance skills and to preparation for internal labor market conditions within the particular occupation or industry with simulations of work rules, experiences, deadlines, and performance requirements on the job. Finally, *employability*, or employment readiness, assesses the individual's attitudes toward the entry-level job; the match between the individual's work habits and internal labor market demands; the individual's willingness to accept supervision; the individual's compatibility with the value systems and work customs within the industry, organization, occupation, and specific work units related to performance on the job; and the individual's attitudes toward work in general.

The requirements of occupations and employers vary widely. Cassell and Cassell (1981) offer a broad view of the technical, professional, adaptive, and social skills required in all jobs. Chapters by Campbell, Kapes and Parrish, and by Nowakowski, Nowakowski, and Lane in this volume all address additional dimensions of this issue from other perspectives. Vocational rehabilitation assessment models offer promising approaches in this area. They use learning samples that ask a person to apply an unfamiliar set of instructions to work-related tasks in a test. Measures of such factors as speed, accuracy, productivity, and capacity to follow and infer work rules and directions are promising approaches to consider.

The ETS tried this approach in a practical reasoning test in its Program for Assessing Youth Employment Skills (PAYES, Educational Testing Service, 1977), an effort recently withdrawn from the market for other reasons. PAYES measured a variety of work adjustment skills—attitudes toward supervision, job-holding skills, job-seeking skills, job knowledge, and self-confidence. While interest in these variables appears to be strong, PAYES measured them only for the lowest-ability youth and failed to link scores with other critical information about the person or the requirements of local employers and industries. These variables remain especially important for any counselor trying to help disadvantaged youth and adults to move from secondary to primary labor market jobs.

Additional elements of such an approach need to assess the job seeker's occupational interests, work experience, and preferences in connection with specific job-related activities, such as those represented in the Interest Checklist of the General Aptitude Test Battery (GATB) and in the DOT; both are available from the U.S. Department of Labor. The job seeker should be encouraged to report interests, skills, and preferences without regard to how or where they were acquired. Skills learned in unpaid jobs, hobbies, community service, informal or self-directed learning, and other settings can all equip a person to meet the requirements of a new job or occupation. Most of the existing computer-assisted career guidance and information systems also rely on the job seeker's preferences for various working conditions, environments, physical demands, training requirements, and other job-specific details to sort and report information to the individual job seeker. Future assessment systems should do no less.

Prescriptive Recommendations and Training. The final dimension needed to match the individual job seeker with the types of employment and training opportunities available in the local job market is to offer the person a range of best-fit recommendations about occupations in which he or she has the best chance for success. The key is to synthesize information about the individual job seeker with employment requirements and training opportunities of specific industries and employers in the local market. The ideal approach seems to be to offer a series of recommendations together with prescriptive and interpretative information that presents a range of opportunities that the person can consider.

One final element that might make such systems especially attractive would be to offer prescriptive profiles of acquired skills and training needs in each of the recommended occupations. Such profiles should reinforce the job-seeker's confidence by highlighting job-relevant skills, and suggesting ways to enable the person to acquire any remaining skills essential to training and job readiness for a particular occupation. Thus, the person would receive suggestions to guide career development planning in each best-fit occupation, including recommendations to improve the person's technical, professional, social, and adaptive skills in areas essential to each of the training and employment opportunities recommended. The individual job seeker and the counselor could then focus on maximizing the net advantage of the job seeker and the potential employer. Once such an assessment and matching resource existed, a variety of program planning and management uses of information about the needs of job seekers, employers, industries, and training organizations in the local job market could unfold. All depend, however, on the existence of strategies and instruments not yet available to individuals, employers, or labor market intermediaries.

Eventually, it may be possible to perform all these assessment and matching functions at computer terminals already linked to state career information and U.S. Employment Service job bank networks. But, until such capabilities are widely available, paper-and-pencil approaches will have to be devised to help achieve the synthesis. Only the test of time and efforts to devise and refine such systems will tell us how far we must still go to meet this challenge.

References

American Psychological Association. *Standards for Educational and Psychological Tests.* Washington, D.C.: American Psychological Association, 1974.

Amundson, N., and Borgen, W. "The Dynamics of Unemployment: Job Loss and Job Search." *Personnel and Guidance Journal,* 1982, *60,* 562–564.

Brenner, M. *Estimating the Social Costs of National Economic Policy: Implications for Mental and Physical Health and Criminal Violence.* Washington, D.C.: U.S. Government Printing Office, 1976.

Bureau of Labor Statistics. *Occupational Projections and Training Data, 1982 Edition.* Washington, D.C.: Bureau of Labor Statistics, 1982.

Carey, M. L. "Evaluating the 1975 Projections of Occupational Employment." *Monthly Labor Review,* 1980, *103* (6), 10–21.

Carey, M. L. "Three Paths to the Future: Occupational Projections, 1980-90." *Occupational Outlook Quarterly,* 1981, *24* (4), 3–11.

Cassell, F. H., and Cassell, E. "'Psyching Out' the Internal Labor Market to Help Improve Job or Career Choice." *International Journal of Manpower,* 1981, *2* (2), 7–18.

Cassell, F. H., Director, S. M., and Doctors, S. I. "Discrimination Within Internal Labor Markets." *Industrial Relations,* 1975, *14* (3), 337–344.

Cassell, F. H., and Rodgers, R. C. "Public and Private Sector Linkages in the Employment and Training System." In F. H. Cassell and others, *Intergovernmental Linkage and Cooperation: Models for Strengthening State and Local Management of Manpower Programs.* Evanston, Ill.: Graduate School of Management, Northwestern University, 1976.

Cassell, F. H., and Rodgers, R. C. "The Public Employment Service as a Labor Market Intermediary." In *Labor Market Intermediaries.* Special Report Number 22. Washington, D.C.: National Commission for Manpower Policy, 1978.

Cassell, F. H., and Rodgers, R. C. "Vocational-Technical Training Initiatives in Economic Development, Employment, and Labor Market Operations." *International Journal of Manpower, 4* (4), in press.

Doeringer, P. B., and Piore, M. J. *Internal Labor Markets and Manpower Analysis.* Lexington, Mass.: Heath, 1971.

Dunn, W. L. "Statewide Career Information Delivery Systems." *Occupational Outlook Quarterly,* 1983, *27* (2), 12–13.

Erikson, E. H. *Childhood and Society.* New York: Norton, 1963.

Educational Testing Service. *Program for Assessing Youth Employment Skills (PAYES).* Princeton, N.J.: Educational Testing Service, 1977.

"ETS to Develop Skills Test Battery for Army." *ETS Developments,* 1982, *28* (1), p. 4.

Freud, S. *Civilization and Its Discontents.* (Trans. J. Strachey.) New York: Norton, 1961.

Ginzberg, E. "Toward a Theory of Occupational Choice—A Restatement." *Vocational Guidance Quarterly,* 1972, *20,* 169–172.

Ginzberg, E., Ginsburg, S. W., Axelrad, S., and Herma, J. L. *Occupational Choice: An Approach to a General Theory.* New York: Columbia University Press, 1951.

Hall, G. S. *Youth: Its Education, Regimen, and Hygiene.* New York: Appleton, 1921.

Havighurst, R. J. *Developmental Tasks and Education.* (3rd ed.) New York: McKay, 1972.

Hecker, D. E. "A Fresh Look at Job Openings." *Occupational Outlook Quarterly,* 1983, *27* (2), 27–29.

Kapes, J. T., and Mastie, M. M. *A Counselor's Guide to Vocational Guidance Instruments.* Alexandria, Va.: National Vocational Guidance Association, 1982.

Kubler-Ross, E. *On Death and Dying.* New York: Macmillan, 1969.

Martin, G. M. "The Job Hunter's Guide to the Library." *Occupational Outlook Quarterly,* 1980, *24* (3), 12–17.

Menninger, K. *Love Against Hate.* New York: Harcourt, Brace and World, 1942.

Miller, A. R., Treiman, D. J., Cain, P. S., and Roos, P. A. (Eds.). *Work, Jobs, and Occupations: A Critical Review of the Dictionary of Occupational Titles.* Washington, D.C.: National Academy Press, 1980.

Parson, M. A., Griffore, R. J., and LaMore, R. L. "Identifying the Needs of Newly Unemployed Workers." *Journal of Employment Counseling,* 1983, *20* (3), 107–113.

Parsons, F. *Choosing a Vocation.* Boston: Houghton-Mifflin, 1909.

Pilot, M. "Job Outlook Projections." *Occupational Outlook Quarterly,* 1980, *24* (4), 3–8.

Rodgers, R. C. "Work Experience as a Mediating Variable in Theories of Occupational Choice." Unpublished doctoral dissertation, Northwestern University, 1975.

Rodgers, R. C. *Educational Planning in the Labor Market: Linking Occupational Education to Regional Economic Development.* Evanston, Ill.: Northwestern University, 1976.

Rodgers, R. C. "A Consumer's Guide to Labor Market Information." In D. H. Salene and M. D. Jacobson (Eds.), *Managing the Life Cycle.* Evanston, Ill.: Northwestern University, 1977.

Rodgers, R. C., and Cassell, F. H. "Southwestern Indiana Employer Survey." Unpublished report to the Vanderburgh County CETA Consortium, Evansville, Ind., 1976.

Rodgers, R. C., and Cassell, F. H. "LaSalle County Employer Survey: Summary Workshop." Unpublished report to the LaSalle County CETA Program, Ottawa, Ill., 1977.

Rugg, E. A. "Limitations of Projections of Occupational Outlook: Users Beware." *Personnel and Guidance Journal,* 1983, *61* (6), 346–349.

Schultz, T. W. *Investment in Human Capital.* New York: Free Press, 1971.

Settles, W. J., Jr. "The Place of Education in Labor Market Operations." Unpublished preliminary doctoral examination, Graduate School of Management, Northwestern University, 1982.

Smith, A. *The Wealth of Nations.* New York: Dutton, 1964. (Originally published 1776).

Stevens, D. W. *Employment Projections for Planning Vocational-Technical Education Curricula: Mission Impossible?* Columbia: University of Missouri, 1976.

Super, D. E. *The Psychology of Careers.* New York: Harper and Brothers, 1957.

Swinburne, P. "The Psychological Impact of Unemployment on Managers and Professional Staff." *Journal of Occupational Psychology,* 1981, *54,* 47–64.

Thorndike, R. L., and Hagan, E. *Ten Thousand Careers.* New York: Wiley, 1959.

Trow, M. "Reflections on Youth Problems and Policies in the United States." In M. S. Gordon and M. Trow (Eds.), *Youth Education and Unemployment Problems: An International Perspective.* Berkeley, Calif.: Carnegie Commission on Policy Studies in Higher Education, 1979.

Turner, C. F. "Using Computers to Match Workers and Jobs: A Preliminary Assessment of the U.S. Employment Service's Automated Matching System." In A. R. Miller, D. J. Treiman, P. S. Cain, and P. A. Roos (Eds.), *Work, Jobs, and Occupations: A Critical Review of the Dictionary of Occupational Titles.* Washington, D.C.: National Academy Press, 1980.

Wirtz, W. W., and the National Manpower Institute. *The Boundless Resource: A Prospectus for an Education-Work Policy.* Washington, D.C.: New Republic, 1975.

Frank H. Cassell is professor of public policy and industrial relations in the Kellogg Graduate School of Management at Northwestern University in Evanston, Illinois. He directed the U.S. Employment Service under President Lyndon B. Johnson.

Ronald C. Rodgers is an assistant director of the Midwestern Field Service Office of the Educational Testing Service in Evanston, Illinois.

Success in a new job or occupation depends on learning how the organization or profession defines competent performance, a concept that needs further attention before we can predict, measure, or facilitate a person's adjustment on the job.

Defining, Measuring, and Facilitating Work Adjustment

Robert E. Campbell

Career development has been conceptualized as consisting of four stages (Campbell and others, 1979; Super and Hall, 1978). These four stages are sequentially defined as the preparation stage — activities related to choosing, preparing for, and entering an occupation; the establishment stage — activities related to demonstrating competence in the occupation and adjusting to the occupational environment; the maintenance stage — activities related to maintaining one's competence in the occupation and to advancing in the occupation; and the retirement stage — activities related to decline in involvement with the occupation. Each stage has associated tasks for successful negotiation of the stage. For example, in the preparation stage, a person needs to choose an occupation; locate, enter, and successfully complete a training program; and subsequently obtain employment in that occupation.

It is not the intent of this chapter to review all four stages comprehensively. Each stage and the relationships among stages can be expanded considerably to illustrate the many ramifications of career development. For example, at the retirement stage, people differ in how they react to formal retirement from a job. Some opt for total leisure. Others view retirement as a transition point that allows them to pursue other career options, such as continuing to

R. C. Rodgers (Ed.). *Measurement Trends in Career and Vocational Education.* New Directions for Testing and Measurement, no. 20. San Francisco: Jossey-Bass, December 1983.

work full-time or part-time in the same occupation, preparing for and entering a new occupation, or reentering the labor force after a period of temporary retirement. People can also recycle through the same stages during their lives as they change occupations before, during, or after reaching the maintenance stage. A common example is women who retire from and return to the labor force periodically while their children are still very young.

The purpose of this chapter is to focus on the establishment stage, giving special attention to the developmental tasks, problems, measurement, and counseling issues associated with it. For the purposes of this chapter, the establishment stage is defined as that in which one demonstrates the ability to function effectively in an occupation. Therefore, this discussion will not include prior activities related to choosing the occupation or to finding a job. The tasks and activities peculiar to the establishment stage have been suggested by the literature on adult and career development and by the literature on organizational and industrial issues. The literature includes commentary by such experts as Dudley and Tiedeman (1977), Gould (1972), Hershenson (1968), Levinson and others (1978), Schein (1978), Stevenson (1977), Super (1963), and Van Maanen (1972).

This literature suggests that the establishment stage is concerned with three activities: socialization, competence, and exploration. Socialization refers to behaviors required to become part of the work environment. It involves adapting to the work setting by learning the rules, procedures, and social patterns of the organization and by establishing relationships to become part of the team. Cassell and Cassell (1981) have referred to this process as "psyching out" the internal labor market. Competence refers to demonstrating that one can perform satisfactorily on the job. Adequate performance involves being adjusted to the work environment, having sufficient motivation, and possessing the necessary skills to accomplish job assignments. Finally, exploration involves the degree to which the person feels that this is the right job or occupation for his or her identity and personal goals. Self-examination can lead the person to explore other job possibilities, both inside and outside the current work environment or in a new occupation. All three activities call for a series of developmental tasks. Figure 1 defines tasks related to these activities and offers examples of each activity. The examples are intended to be representative rather than exhaustive.

Figure 1. Establishment Stage Tasks

Goal: To demonstrate initially one's ability to function effectively in an occupation

Task I: To become oriented to the organization/institution (socialization)
  A. Learn the way around the physical plant
  B. Learn and adhere to regulations and policies
  C. Learn the formal and informal structure of the work environment
    1. Learn and utilize appropriate channels of communication

    D. Learn and use environmental resources appropriately

    E. Learn and display good work habits and attitudes

    F. Develop harmonious relationships with others in the work environment

       1. Learn and demonstrate expected social behavior

       2. Achieve acceptance of others in the work environment

       3. Develop a personal support system inside the work environment

    G. Display flexibility in adapting to organizational/institutional changes

    H. Integrate personal values with organizational/institutional values

Task II: To learn position responsibilities and demonstrate satisfactory performance (competence)

    A. Use previously acquired skills in position performance as appropriate

    B. Learn how to use job-related equipment, materials, and resources

    C. Acquire new skills as tasks of position change

       1. Take part in on-the-job training as appropriate

    D. Learn formal and informal quality and level of productivity

    E. Demonstrate adequate position performance to others in the work environment

    F. Experience self-confidence in position performance

Task III: Explore career plans in terms of personal goals and advancement opportunities (exploration)

    A. Evaluate current choice of occupation

       1. Determine match between personal attributes and requirements of current position

       2. Assess potential of current position for satisfying personal needs

    B. Evaluate advancement opportunities of current position

       1. Know the requirements for advancement

       2. Assess personal capacity to meet requirements for advancement

    C. Develop a plan for advancement or position change

       1. Survey internal and external organizational/institutional opportunities

       2. Decide on specialization within current occupation

       3. Consider alternatives in other occupations

    D. Implement plan for advancement or position change

Source: Campbell and others, 1979, p. 30–31.

Problems occur when an individual experiences difficulty in coping with one or more of the career development tasks listed in Figure 1. Success in an occupation depends on learning to adhere to organizational regulations and policies, to display of good work habits, and to use of job-related equipment, materials, and resources.

Over the past ten to fifteen years, employers have demonstrated an increased interest in assisting employees with their occupational well-being and career development. A number of companies have established career development programs to improve morale and use of resources (Lancaster and Berne, 1981). These programs vary in the range of services offered. Services range from minimal orientation to the work setting to in-depth job adjustment counseling and career planning.

Measuring Adjustment

Approaches to measuring the degree of adjustment during occupational establishment have for the most part used traditional instruments — primarily job satisfaction and performance measures — to focus on various aspects of this stage. However, a number of other behaviors could also be measured, including mentoring, the socialization process, stress, organizational commitment, and career exploration and planning. Each of these behaviors will be discussed briefly in the paragraphs that follow.

Mentoring is the support that an established worker or supervisor gives to help a neophyte to become established. Mentoring can include a variety of supportive behaviors, such as providing a role model and being an advocate, teacher, confidant, morale booster, rules interpreter, encourager, and social liaison.

Socialization is the process by which a new employee is assimilated into the organization. During the process, the employee develops a sense of identity, belonging, mutual acceptance, integration, and contribution to the organization.

Job stress refers to conditions on the job that produce individual strain, which is usually manifested by physical or psychological symptoms, such as tension, depression, and sleeping disorders. Osipow and Spokane (1981) have developed a set of three instruments to assess occupational stress, strain, and coping.

Organizational commitment refers to the degree to which an employee shares the organization's values and goals. Although it can be part of the socialization process, commitment can also represent more than assimilation into the organization, since it suggests a more intensive personal identity with the organization.

Career exploration and planning refers to the amount of self-examination in which the employee has engaged in order to assess his or her status in the current position. This self-examination includes consideration of the degree of satisfaction with the present position as weighed against personal career goals and exploration of other career opportunities both inside and outside the organization. In addition, the occupationally established employee may consider the possibilities of other occupations if the present occupation is not meeting his or her needs and goals.

Several pilot instruments have been developed to assess the multiple tasks of occupational establishment. These include the Adaptation to Work Questionnaire (Ashley and others, 1980) and the Career Adjustment and Development Inventory (Crites, 1979). The Adaptation to Work Questionnaire measures five aspects of work adaptation: organizational, performance, interpersonal, responsibility, and affective. The questionnaire was pilot tested with sixty-eight men and women between eighteen and thirty years of age who had less than a college degree and who had been working in a full-time job for no more than nine months. The five subscales were highly correlated with one another and with total scale score. The authors concluded that the five scales represented two major factors: the first contained items indirectly related to a job, while the second factor reflected items related to job performance.

The Career Adjustment and Development Inventory (CAR-ADI) was constructed to measure how well employees were accomplishing the career development tasks of the establishment stage. The CAR-ADI consists of six scales that measure career choice and plans, career advancement, position performance, work habits and attitudes, organizational adaptability, and co-worker relationships. The instrument was pilot tested on 110 employees from three industries. Their average age was 34.7, and there were roughly equal numbers of males and females. The respondents had worked an average of 14.8 years. They had job titles ranging from management to maintenance, production, and support services. Pilot findings indicated that the items showed both a group and a general factor of career development task mastery during the establishment stage. Additionally, more than half of the items correlated moderately with a job satisfaction measure.

Recommendations for Research and Measurement

This brief review of occupational entry and establishment generates a wide range of possible research and measurement issues on which future efforts can focus. Although there are a number of approaches to examining the issues, it may be helpful to categorize the issues into three broad foci of adjustment to occupational entry and establishment: predicting adjustment, measuring adjustment, and facilitating adjustment.

Predicting Adjustment. What variables are most likely to predict satisfactory adjustment? The possibilities include previous work experience, appropriateness of occupational choice, personality characteristics, job coping and survival skills, adequacy of technical training, adequacy of basic academic skills, knowledge of career planning techniques and resources, and work habits and attitudes.

Measuring Adjustment. The two multidimensional instruments described previously, the Adaptation to Work Questionnaire and the Career Adjustment and Development Inventory, appear to represent promising approaches to measuring the key tasks of this stage of career development as gross indexes of adjustment.

However, to be optimally useful, measures of adjustment should not only provide information about the degree of adjustment but also be diagnostically prescriptive in giving clues about interventions needed to improve adjustment. For example, if a person is having difficulty adapting to the organization, it would be useful if the specific aspect of organizational adaptability could be identified. This aspect could be a clash of values, difficulty in understanding organizational procedures, or knowledge of communication channels. Diagnostic information can also be useful to the organization by providing patterns or profiles of adjustment among workers that allow it to take corrective action, such as training, improving physical facilities, or establishing a career development program.

Consequently, it is recommended that further research in this area should be concerned with the development of instruments that have diagnostic utility. Both instruments cited here have diagnostic potential through further refinement of their scales. Additionally, other unidimensional instruments could be developed to assess specific dimensions (tasks) of this career development stage.

Facilitating Adjustment. What factors are most likely to facilitate or to impede adjustment? Facilitating factors include the opportunity to upgrade academic basic skills or technical skills, mentoring, co-worker support networks, career development counseling, and professional growth and support networks external to the organization, such as professional associations, trade unions, and family.

Factors that impede adjustment tend to be the reverse of facilitating factors, such as lack of opportunities to upgrade skills, failure to use co-worker support networks, adverse off-the-job stressors that impede work performance, and ambiguous job assignments.

References

Ashley, W. L., and others. *Adaptation to Work: An Exploration of Processes and Outcomes.* Columbus, Ohio: National Center for Research in Vocational Education, 1980.

Campbell, R. E., and Heffernan, J. M. "Adult Vocational Behavior." In W. B. Walsh and S. H. Osipow (Eds.), *Handbook of Vocational Psychology.* Vol. 1. Hillsdale, N.J.: Erlbaum, 1983.

Campbell, R. E., and others. A Diagnostic Taxonomy of Adult Career Problems. Columbus, Ohio: National Center for Research in Vocational Education, 1979.

Cassell, F. H., and Cassell, E. "'Psyching Out' the Internal Labor Market to Help Improve Job or Career Choice." *International Journal of Manpower,* 1981, *2* (2), 7–18.

Crites, J. O. "Validation of the Diagnostic Taxonomy of Adult Career Problems." In R. E. Campbell and others, *A Diagnostic Taxonomy of Adult Career Problems.* Columbus, Ohio: National Center for Research in Vocational Education, 1979.

Dudley, G. A., and Tiedeman, D. V. *Career Development: Exploration and Commitment.* Muncie, Ind.: Accelerated Development, 1977.

Gould, R. "The Phases of Adult Life: A Study in Developmental Psychology." *American Journal of Psychiatry,* 1972, *29,* 521–531.

Hershenson, D. B. "Life-Stage Vocational Development System." *Journal of Counseling Psychology,* 1968, *15,* 23–30.

Lancaster, A., and Berne, R. *Employer-Sponsored Career Development Programs.* Information Series No. 231. Columbus, Ohio: National Center for Research in Vocational Education, 1981.

Levinson, D. J., Darrow, C. N., Klein, E. B., Levinson, M. H., and McKee, B. *The Seasons of a Man's Life.* New York: Knopf, 1978.

Osipow, S. H., and Spokane, A. R. *A Preliminary Manual for Measures of Occupational Stress, Strain, and Coping.* Columbus, Ohio: Marathon Consulting and Press, 1981.

Schein, E. H. *Career Dynamics: Matching Individual and Organizational Needs.* Reading, Mass.: Addison-Wesley, 1978.

Stevenson, J. L. *Issues and Crises During Middlescence.* New York: Appleton-Century-Crofts, 1977.

Super, D. E. "Vocational Development in Adolescence and Early Adulthood: Tasks and Behaviors." In D. E. Super, R. Starishevsky, N. Matlin, and J. P. Jordaan (Eds.), *Career Development: Self-Concept Theory.* Monograph No. 4. New York: College Entrance Examination Board, 1963.

Super, D. E., and Hall, D. T. "Career Development: Exploration and Planning." *Annual Review of Psychology,* 1978, *29,* 333–372.

Van Maanen, J. "Breaking In: A Consideration of Organizational Socialization." Technical Report No. 10. Irvine: Graduate School of Administration, University of California, 1972.

Robert E. Campbell is a senior research specialist at the National Center for Research in Vocational Education and a professor of psychology at the Ohio State University, Columbus.

*Public Law 94–142 has brought national attention to career guidance
and assessment for the handicapped, but practitioners still seek
advice about assessment tools and how the resulting information
enhances job training and placement for their clients.*

Career Guidance and Assessment Tools for Handicapped Persons

Jerome T. Kapes
Linda H. Parrish

Handicapped people do not form a single homogeneous group. Thus, it may be helpful to begin this discussion by clarifying definitions of who they are and how various approaches to career assessment are responsive to their special needs. Classifications are imperfect, however, because each person is unique. Classifications must be used cautiously, and they cannot substitute for sensitivity to the uniqueness of the individuals. The benefit of classification is that it focuses on particular types of handicapping conditions and suggests adjustments that can improve the usefulness of career assessment for many individuals.

Too often, the education system views the handicapped as a class of mildly to moderately retarded students. Often, the members of this class are referred to as educable mentally retarded (EMR) youth. While it is true that this group makes up a large subset of the handicapped persons served in schools, there are many other handicapped persons who also should be considered.

Eleven handicapping conditions are defined by Public Law 94–142, the Education for All Handicapped Children Act of 1975. Two criteria must be met according to the federal legislation: First, students must be evaluated and found to have one or more of the eleven handicapping conditions. Second,

R. C. Rodgers (Ed.). *Measurement Trends in Career and Vocational Education.* New Directions
for Testing and Measurement, no. 20. San Francisco: Jossey-Bass, December 1983.

students must require special education services to overcome these impairments. Not all handicapped students need or receive special services. Obviously, assessment is an essential part of identifying handicapped students and of determining how to meet their needs. The Office of Education (1977) identified the eleven handicapping conditions as follows:

1. *Mental Retardation* — significantly subaverage intellectual development and functioning coupled with adaptive behavior deficits.

2. *Specific Learning Disability* — a disorder that affects the ability to understand and use written or spoken language. This condition is not caused by a sensory loss, such as visual or hearing impairments.

3. *Orthopedic Impairment* — a physical disability caused by congenital anomaly, disease, or accident resulting in absence, modification, or loss of control of muscle function.

4. *Serious Emotional Disturbance* — an unexplained inability to learn, maintain relationships, or predict behavior under normal circumstances. These symptoms must be exhibited over a long period of time and to a marked degree.

5. *Deafness* — a severe hearing impairment.

6. *Hearing Impairment* — a hearing impairment that inhibits the student's performance.

7. *Deafness and Blindness* — the combination of the two severe impairments.

8. *Visual Handicap* — includes partially sighted and blind persons.

9. *Speech Impairment* — a communication disorder such as stuttering, articulation inaccuracy, or language/voice disorder.

10. *Other Health Impairment* — an inability to perform because of limited strength or alertness due to a health-related condition.

11. *Multihandicappedness* — the combination of two or more handicapping conditions.

Each of these eleven conditions is defined in relationship to its effect on educational performance. It is important to remember that it is possible for an individual to have an identified handicapping condition and not to require special services. If one understands this concept, then it becomes easier to accept the fact that career assessment, as well as curricula modifications, should be undertaken only to the extent necessary to enable each individual to participate fully in the educational process.

In addition to defining who the handicapped are, it will also be useful to clarify the notion of career guidance and assessment tools. For the purpose of this chapter, we use the phrase *career guidance and assessment tools* as a generic term for what is often referred to in the literature as *vocational evaluation* or *vocational assessment.* According to Nadolsky (1981, p. 6), "vocational evaluation is a specialized type of vocational guidance service designed to assist individuals with special needs in determining their vocational potential. . . . It is the experiential phase of vocational evaluation and its practical, realistic work-related techniques and procedures provide the core content for vocational evaluation and set it apart from traditional programs of vocational assessment and guidance."

Both the term *vocational evaluation* and many of its techniques were developed by those who worked with adults in the field of vocational rehabilitation. When it became apparent that the public schools needed to provide a free and appropriate education to all handicapped youth, many methods of vocational rehabilitation were adapted for that part of the appropriate education that had to do with preparation for employment (Krantz, 1979). In adopting and adapting the methods of vocational rehabilitation, public school educators chose the term *vocational assessment* to refer to their version of the individual evaluation process. Salvia and Ysseldyke (1978), Albright and others (1978), Sitlington (1980), and Peterson (1981) all use the term to indicate appraisal of a student's vocational potential.

The term *career* is used in preference to *vocational* in the title of this chapter as a modifer for *guidance and assessment* because it has greater breadth and scope and because the purpose of assessment is to appraise potential for work. Although we agree with the distinction between career and vocation proposed by Hoyt (1974), they are not greatly different for the purposes of this chapter, and we use them interchangeably.

Legislation and Policies

Over the past decade, the legislation dealing with the rights of handicapped individuals has proliferated. In concert, these acts have created a significant emphasis on providing appropriate educational experiences for students who had not been served or who had been served inadequately in the past. The most important legislation for this topic is the Vocational Rehabilitation Act of 1973 (Public Law 93–112), the Education for All Handicapped Children Act of 1975 (Public Law 94–142), Title II of the Education Amendments of 1976 (Public Law 94–482), and the Office of Civil Rights (OCR) (Office of Civil Rights, 1979) vocational education programs guidelines.

One major theme is common to all. The Vocational Rehabilitation Act of 1973 prohibits discrimination against handicapped persons in regard to employment, education, program accessibility, health, welfare, or social services. The Office of Civil Rights (1979) guidelines address vocational counseling of handicapped persons as it pertains to admission criteria, recruitment, and placement into vocational programs (Kapes and Greenwood, 1979). The Education for all Handicapped Children Act of 1975 states specific guidelines to assure basic rights for handicapped students regarding testing and evaluation procedures. In addition to providing for full evaluation of a student's educational needs before the student is placed in a special education program, P.L. 94–142 insists that tests and evaluation materials should not be racially or culturally discriminating, they should not be merely single tests of intelligence, and they should not be discriminatory because of the student's handicap. Moreover, the materials should be administered in the student's primary mode of communication, they should be validated for the purpose for which they are used, they should be administered by trained personnel, and they should be evaluated by a multidisciplinary team. Title II of the Education Amendments of 1976 addresses vocational education. It reinforces the other assurances by requiring vocational programming in each state to be consistent with the state plans required by P.L. 94–142. This regulation enhances support by ensuring that 10 percent of vocational funding is spent for services that are in excess of expenditures for the nonhandicapped student.

This legislation has many implications for those involved in career guidance and assessment. It is imperative for assessment to be sensitive to a student's disability so that the handicap does not bias his or her performance. Some instruments can be used with no modification, but others may require adjustments, such as special answer sheets, longer time periods, or interpreters. Finally, some tests and inventories may not be useful at all with certain populations. For example, a student with limited mobility and manual dexterity may be unable to complete physical manipulation tasks in a work sample, and a hearing-impaired student cannot compete fairly on a test of sound discrimination or listening skills. In situations like these, assessment tools must be sensitive to the special needs of the individual student to assure that what is measured is valid, fair, and appropriate for the individual.

Career Development of the Handicapped

In most respects, career development of the handicapped is not different from career development for people in general. Clark (1980, p. 15) makes the point that "a developmental approach to establishing a rationale for career education programming for the handicapped is justified by the delayed, disordered, or uneven development in learning skills for daily living, personal-social, school, or occupational activities among handicapped children and youth." This position, with which we agree, suggests that the vocational theories proposed by Ginzberg and others (1951) and by Super and others (1957) also apply to the handicapped. These theories need to be applied differently to the extent that the particular handicapping condition interferes with the developmental tasks to be accomplished.

Brolin and Kokaska (1979) take a traditional approach to career education by defining four stages of career development: career awareness; career exploration; career preparation; and career placement, follow-up, and continuing education. The competencies that must be attained during these stages are defined in three broad categories of daily living skills, personal-social skills, and occupational guidance and preparation. In contrast, Clark (1980) focuses on four developmental areas: values, attitudes, and habits; human relationships; occupational information; and acquisition of actual job and daily living skills. From the perspective of these two approaches, it is evident that much of the school curriculum for the handicapped is devoted to work and life adjustment skills as well as to cognitive capacity and affective orientation for work. A second major theme of the literature on handicapped persons is that mastery of these skills can be expected to occur at a slower rate or to a lesser degree for some but not all handicapped people. It is the true function of vocational assessment of the handicapped to ascertain the rate and amount of development that has occurred or that can occur in the several areas just described.

A Three-Level Model of Vocational Assessment

Given the federal incentives to conduct vocational assessment, some states have taken the initiative in developing guidelines for implementing a comprehensive evaluation system. The comprehensive Texas model (Texas Education Agency, 1980) has proven effective in practice. The discussion that follows adapts many elements of its approach to vocational assessment. The Texas model, as modified by the writers, contains three levels of assessment information: Level I information includes special education data; information acquired from interviews with student, parents, and teachers; and information from review of cumulative school records. Level II information includes level I information and information from vocational aptitude tests, vocational interests and values inventories, and work adjustment competencies measures. Level III information includes level I and level II information plus information from work samples, vocational course tryout, and job tryout.

This model allows appropriate educational placement decisions to be made at each level while providing for a more in-depth evaluation if it is required. The procedure aids in determining which students can benefit from vocational education and which occupational areas should be investigated prior to placement. As with all evaluation of handicapped students, the process should serve not to screen handicapped students out of skills training programs but to determine appropriate vocational placement.

Level I Assessment. The special education data typically found in the files of handicapped students consist of reports on such factors as language, emotional and behavioral development, intelligence, physical development, and academic development. The review will include results of standard speech, vision, and audiology tests as well as results on such educational performance tests as the Wide Range Achievement Test (WRAT). Social and developmental ratings may be available on standardized instruments, such as the Vineland Social Maturity Scale, the Brigance Test of Essential Skills, and the American Association of Mental Deficiencies (AAMD) Adaptive Behavioral Scales. Results of tests assessing physical strength and the Purdue Pegboard or Minnesota Rate of Manipulation Test to determine dexterity are also typical of data found in this category.

Interviews with student, parents, and teachers are the second type of level I data. From the student, helpful information can be obtained regarding career expectations and attitudes toward vocational education and work in general. Parents can corroborate this information and provide additional information about interests and work habits at home. Teachers of both academic and prevocational courses can attest to work-relevant attitudes and habits as well as to aptitude and interests.

Cumulative school records provide data that can be invaluable for determining vocational options. Such information includes I.Q. test results, attendance patterns, grades, and disciplinary actions. Intelligence tests that have both verbal and performance components, such as the Wechsler Intelligence Scale for Children (WISC-R) or the Wechsler Adult Intelligence Scale (WAIS), are often used in this manner. The Slosson Intelligence Test, a verbal I.Q. test that requires no reading, is often a part of the cumulative record for students who have a reading handicap.

If a vocational placement decision cannot be made after examining all the data available for level I assessment, then additional information can be obtained through formal assessment as described in level II.

Level II Assessment. A number of guides have been developed to help with selection of instruments for use in what we have characterized as level II assessment. Kapes and Mastie (1982), Grisafe (1983) and Getzel and Tindall (1983) provide examples of these guides that are all very useful. Three types of information are most useful for level II assessment: information on aptitudes and basic skills (what the person can learn or what the person has learned that is basic to future learning), information on interests and work values (what the person likes to do or values doing), and information on work adjustment competencies (attitudes and behaviors that contribute to success on the job).

Aptitudes and basic skills are ascertained to some degree in level I assessment, but they need to be reassessed in the present because they continue to develop and because of their specific relationship to work and work training. Getzel and Tindall (1983) define five categories of skill competencies: quantitative and numerical skills, verbal skills, perceptual skills, language skills, and psychomotor skills.

Interests and work values are placed together, but they approach the individual's affective orientation to work from different perspectives. Interests are work preferences stated in terms of activities, while work values are reinforcements or needs that one hopes to satisfy from work. Measures of interest can be given as homogeneous clusters (for example, outdoor, mechanical, social, artistic) or as empirical similarities between a person and a group of persons working in an occupation who are successful and satisfied (for example, auto mechanics, accountants, nurses, school teachers). Work values are generic. They are thought to be outer manifestations of inner needs (Katz, 1963) (for example, salary, recognition, prestige, achievement).

Work adjustment competencies are largely affective, but they incorporate aptitude and basic skills into self-concept as it relates to work. They are skills, and they have a cognitive component, but they are mediated through the affective self. These competencies may in fact be the difference between those who succeed on the job and those who do not. They are what employers are always telling educators (especially vocational educators) they want taught, but they are also the skills or attitudes that we know the least about teaching. Getzel and Tindall (1983) list four categories containing these competencies: job readiness competencies, work attitude competencies, work performance competencies, and work tolerance competencies.

Table 1 lists, briefly describes, and comments on instruments that can be useful in obtaining data for each of the three areas of information included in level II assessment. Further information on many of the instruments included in Table 1 is available in Kapes and Mastie (1982).

Level III Assessment. Vocational assessment of the type described in this section is employed after level II assessment and on an as needed basis. This is not to imply that a person needs to have a greater handicap in order to qualify for level III assessment but only that there needs to be a clear reason for prescribing it. Although level III consists of three different types of measures or experiences, all three types do not need to be employed.

Of the three types of measures, work samples most nearly represent assessment of a classical measurement nature applied to a clinical behavior sample. According to the Texas Education Agency (1980, p. 12) guidelines, work samples are "tasks or activities that simulate a specific job and [that] are used to assess skills, aptitudes, and abilities similar to those required in competitive employment situations." Although a great deal of training and experience is required to administer work samples correctly, they vary considerably from specific job elements to general career cluster exploratory activities. From a psychometric point of view, most commerically available work samples are still quite crude, and in many cases the data on norms, reliability, and validity are inadequate. Table 2 lists most of the commercially available work samples together with publisher information and a brief description and comments on use. Botterbusch (1980) can provide more information on most of the work samples listed here.

Beyond the commercially available work samples, there is still much room for locally developed work samples. In fact, it is likely that a locally developed work sample constructed and administered by the vocational teacher who will teach the student for whom the assessment is conducted will be more content-valid than any work sample that can be purchased. This does not eliminate the need for obtaining measurement data, and it is recommended that those who develop their own work samples work closely with a professional educator trained in measurement techniques.

Vocational course tryout is one step removed from locally developed work samples, and it may be preferable when circumstances permit, since there is probably no better way of finding out whether a person can learn a vocational skill and whether the person is interested in learning that skill than to give the person a chance to give it a try. In this approach, exploration and

Table 1. Instruments that May Be Useful for Level II Vocational Assessment of Handicapped Students

Type/Name	Publisher	Description & Comments on Use
Aptitude/Basic Skill		
Adult Basic Learning Exam (ABLE)	The Psychological Corporation	Measures learning ability of non-completing high school students. Gives scores for vocabulary, reading, spelling and arithmetic. High school-adults.
Appraisal of Occupational Aptitudes	Riverside Publishing Company	Used for selection and counseling regarding business and office careers. Grade 9-adults.
Basic Occupational Literacy Test (BOLT)	U.S. Government Printing Office	Assesses basic skills in reading comprehension, vocabulary, arithmetic computation and reasoning. Grades 1-11.
Bennett Hand-Tool Dexterity Test	The Psychological Corporation	Measures manual dexterity and gross motor coordination while using tools. High school-adults.
Career Ability Placement Survey (CAPS)	Educational and Industrial Testing Service (EdITS)	Measures abilities keyed to entry requirements for the majority of jobs within 14 occupational clusters. Grades 7-adults.
Clerical Skills Series	Martin M. Bruce Publishers	Reports scores on clerical skills such as filing and punctuation. Clerical workers and applicants.
Comprehensive Ability Battery	Institute of Personality and Ability Testing	Twenty sub-tests some of which include rote memory, spelling, originality, and mechanical ability. Ages 15-over.
Crawford Small Parts Dexterity Text	The Psychological Corporation	Measures fine finger dexterity and eye-hand coordination while manipulating tweezers and pins. High school and adults.
Dailey Vocational Tests	Riverside Publishing Company	Examines potential for a wide range of occupations in trade, technical, and business-secretarial fields. Grade 8-adults.
Differential Aptitude Test (DAT)	The Psychological Corporation	Designed for educational and vocational guidance in Jr. and Sr. high schools. Nine scores include mechanical reasoning and space relations. Grades 8-12.
Flanagan Industrial Tests	Science Research Associates, Inc.	Eighteen short tests which include assembly, electronics, and vocabulary. Seven tests are entry level specific. Non-college adults.
General Aptitude Test Battery (GATB)	U.S. Government Printing Office	Measures nine major aptitudes required for occupational success. Used by U.S. Employment Service. Grades 9-12 and adults.
Minnesota Clerical Test	The Psychological Corporation	A test of speed and accuracy in performing tasks such as number and name checking. Grades 8-12 and adults.
Minnesota Rate of Manipulation Test	American Guidance Service, Inc.	Assesses arm-hand dexterity. Requires placement, turning and displacing of cylinders into holes. Grades 7-adults, plus norms for blind persons.
Minnesota Spatial Relations Test	American Guidance Service, Inc.	Requires the transfer of 58 blocks of assorted sizes and shapes from one board to another. Ages 11 and over.
Nonreading Aptitude Test Battery (NATB)	U.S. Government Printing Office	A non-reading alternative to the GATB. Useful in vocational counseling with educationally deficient students. Grade 9-adults.
O'Connor Finger Dexterity Test	Stoelting Company	Assesses motor coordination and manual dexterity. Metal pins are inserted in holes as rapidly as possible. Ages 14 and over.
O'Connor Tweezer Dexterity Test	Stoelting Company	Assesses motor coordination and manual dexterity. Metal pins are inserted in holes with use of tweezers. Ages 14 and over.
Pennsylvania Bi-Manual Worksample	American Guidance Service, Inc.	Requires assembly and disassembly of nuts and bolts as it measures hand and finger dexterity. Ages 16 and over.
Purdue Pegboard	Science Research Associates, Inc.	Measures manual dexterity using a board, pins, washers and collars. Grades 9-adults.
Short Occupational Knowledge Tests	Science Research Associate, Inc.	Twelve Tests measure content knowledge in such occupations as carpenter, secretary, and welder. Adults.
Short Test of Clerical Ability	Science Research Associate, Inc.	Measures seven areas associated with clerical work for use in job placement. Applicants for office positions.

Type/Name	Publisher	Description & Comments on Use
SRA Test of Mechanical Concepts	Science Research Associate, Inc.	Used to evaluate for hire, promotion or training for mechanical jobs such as assembler or machinist. Grades 8–adults.
Stromberg Dexterity Test	The Psychological Corporation	Assesses speed and accuracy of arm and hand movement. Used by trade schools with adults.
Tests of Adult Basic Education (TABE)	CTB/McGraw-Hill	Establishes a level at which instruction should begin in basic skills. Analyzes the needs of adults who wish to pursue vocational training or general literacy study. Adults.
Word and Number Assessment Inventory	NCS Interpretive Scoring System	Measures verbal and mathematical ability and compares them with educational and occupational groups. Grades 9–adults.

Interests/Work Values

Type/Name	Publisher	Description & Comments on Use
AAMD–Becker Reading-Free Vocational Interest Inventory	American Association on Mental Deficiency	A non-reading vocational preference inventory for mentally retarded people at the unskilled and semiskilled levels. High school EMR.
Applied Biological and Agribusiness Interest Inventory	Interstate Printers & Publishers, Inc.	Identifies students with high interest in vocational agriculture fields. Grade 8.
California Life Goals Evaluation Schedules	Western Psychological Services	An inventory based on ten career value areas such as fame, security, and independence. Ages 15 and over.
California Occupational Preference System (COPS)	Educational & Industrial Testing Service (EdITS)	Mesures job activity interests in 14 general interest areas such as outdoor, clerical and arts. Middle school–adults.
Career Assessment Inventory (CAI)	NCS Interpretive Scoring Systems	An interest inventory that compares interests to those of workers in occupations requiring less than a college education. Grade 8–adults.
Career Guidance Inventory	Educational Guidance, Inc.	Designed for counseling students with interests in trades, services and technology. Grades 7–13.
Career Orientation Placement and Evaluation Survey (COPES)	Educational & Industrial Testing Service (EdITS)	Measurement of personal values representing the vocational motivation or value domain. Grades 7–12, college, and adults.
Geist Picture Interest Inventory	Western Psychological Service	Uses pictures to obtain 11 interest scores such as mechanical or literary and seven motivational scores such as prestige and environmental. Male and female versions.
Geist Picture Interest Inventory (Deaf Form)	Western Psychological Service	Reports 10 interest scales omitting musical from the original Geist instrument. Deaf and hard of hearing males, grades 7–16 and adults.
Gordon Occupational Check List	The Psychological Corporation	An interest checklist covering 240 jobs not requiring college training. Grades 8–adults.
Hall Occupational Orientation Inventroy	Scholastic Testing Service, Inc.	An instructional package in a measurement format. Aids in recognizing occupational values and needs. Grades 3–college and reading handicapped adults.
Harrington–O'Shea Career Decision-Making System	American Guidance Service, Inc.	A self-assessment and interest inventory that provides detailed occupational information. Grade 7–adults.
How Well Do You Know Your Interests?	Edupac, Inc.	Collects information about students likes and dislikes of jobs, activities, people, and things. High school and college.
Interest Determination, Exploration and Assessment System (IDEAS)	NCS Interpretive Scoring System	A self-contained, self-scoring interest inventory consisting of 14 scales such as electronics, science, writing and sales. Grades 6–12.
Jackson Vocational Interest Survey	Research Psychologists Press, Inc.	Consists of 34 basic interest scales that assist in college and career planning. High school–adults for college level careers.
Job Attitude Scale	Shoukry D. Sahel	Deals with 17 intrinsic and extrinsic factors in job satisfaction and motivation such as salary and recognition. Adults.
Judgement of Occupational Behavior-Orientation (JOB-O)	CFKR Career Materials, Inc.	Assists in narrowing job titles to those that best match personal needs through preference testing. Grade 7–adults.

Table 1. Instruments that May Be Useful for Level II
Vocational Assessment of Handicapped Students *(continued)*

Type/Name	Publisher	Description & Comments on Use
Kuder General Interest Survey (Form E)	Science Research Associates, Inc.	Measures 10 broad vocational interests such as outdoor, mechanical, and artistic for use in counseling and career exploration. Grades 6-12.
Kuder Occupational Interest Survey (FORM DD)	Science Research Associates, Inc.	Measures 126 occupational scales and 48 college major scales for use in counseling college bound. Grade 11-adults.
Minnesota Importance Questionnaire (MIQ)	Vocational Psychology Research	Measures 20 psychological needs relevant to work satisfaction. Ages 16 and over.
Missouri Occupational Card Sort	Career Planning and Placement Service	Expands the range of occupations being considered and encourages further career exploration. Grades 11-adults.
Missouri Occupational Preference Inventory	Human Systems Consultants, Inc.	A card sort which assists in exploring career options and understanding career choice. High school-adults.
Non-Sexist Vocational Card Sort	NSVCS, C. R. Dewey	A card sort which explores feeling and values which limit the options that vocational clients perceive as being open to them. High school-adults.
OCC-U-Sort	Publishers Test Service	A card sort designed to stimulate career exploration, examine motives for occupational choice and broaden career options. Junior high school-adults.
Ohio Vocational Interest Survey (OVIS II)	The Psychological Corporation	Consists of 23 scales based on data, people and things such as agriculture and medical. To assist students with vocational planning. Grade 8-adults.
Picture Interest Exploration Survey	Education Achievement Corporation	A career interest inventory using 156 slides. Includes 13 areas such as office and construction work using workers' hands in each slide. Grades 7-12.
Self Description Inventory	NCS Interpretive Scoring Systems	Relates 11 personality scales to career choice. Holland's six types are used. Grades 9-adults.
Self Directed Search (SDS)	Consulting Psychologists Press, Inc.	A self administered, scored and interpreted vocational counseling tool that encourages the exploration of careers. Junior high school-adults.
Strong-Campbell Interest Inventory (SCII)	Stanford University Press	Provides a comparative measure of one's interest to people in general and people in a wide variety of professional occupations. Grades 8-adults.
Temperament and Values Inventory (TVI)	NCS Interpretive Scoring Systems	Temperament scales describe how one reacts in various situations while the reward values scale measures what parts of a job may be rewarding. Grades 9-adults.
USES Interest Inventory	U.S. Government Printing Office	Provides measures of occupational interest in occupations that have been classified in the USES Guide for Occupational Exploration. High school-adults.
Vocational Exploration and Insight Kit	Consulting Psychologist Press, Inc.	Uses a card sort to encourage self exploration. Based on Holland's Self Directed Search. High school-adults.
Vocational Interest, Experience and Skill Assessment (VIESA)	The Riverside Publishing Company	Develops self awareness while exploring over 650 career options. Grades 8-12.
Vocational Interest and Sophistication Assessment	O.S.U. Nisonger Center	A reading free picture instrument that measures one's interest and knowledge about unskilled and semi-skilled jobs. Mildly retarded adolescents-adults.
Wide Range Interest-Opinion Test (WRIOT)	Jastak Associates, Inc.	Determines interests and attitudes about jobs regardedless of age, sex, mental ability, cultural background or educational level. Age 5-adults.
What I Like to Do	Science Research Associates, Inc.	Helps children identify interests, curricular and career preferences. Grades 4-7.
Work Values Inventory (WVI)	The Riverside Publishing Co.	Self report inventory designed to measure 15 satisfactions (values) that people seek in their work. Grades 7-12-adults.

Work Adjustment Competencies

AAMD Adaptive Behavior Scale	American Association of Mental Deficiency	Assesses the effectiveness of an individual in coping with the natural and social demands of the environment. Primarily for mentally retarded.
Career Awareness Inventory	Scholastic Testing Service, Inc.	Assesses overall occupational awareness and evaluates the effectiveness of instructional programs. Elementary-high school.

Type/Name	Publisher	Description & Comments on Use
Career Decision Scale	Marathon Consulting & Press	An 18 item rating scale designed to identify barriers preventing one from making career descisions. Grades 9-college.
Career Development Inventory (CDI)	Consulting Psychologists Press	Assesses the readiness to make pre-occupational and vocational decisions in terms of attitudes, knowledge and skills. Junior high school-college.
Career Education Readiness Test	Career Education Readiness Measurement & Research	Measures knowledge and attitude regarding vocational concepts such as work vocabulary and sex role stereotyping. Grades K-6.
Career Maturity Inventory (CMI)	CTB/McGraw-Hill	Consists of five competence scales and an attitude scale that provides information important for mature career decision-making. Grades 6-12.
Career Skills Assessment Program (CSAP)	The College Board	Evaluates the extent to which students have mastered fundamental career development principles. Grade 9-adults.
Employment Readiness Scale	Anthony M. Alfano	Measures a person's readiness for work by assessing work values. Beneficial for un, semi or skilled work settings. High school-adults.
Experience Exploration	Chronicle Guidance	A career decision model based on evaluation of experience. Relates self-assessed experiences to the world of work. Grades 9-14.
Individual Career Exploration	Scholastic Testing Service	Consists of both picture and verbal forms that measures interests, abilities, experiences and occupational choices. Grades 3-12.
Knowledge of Occupations Test	Edupac, Inc.	Measures student information about careers in terms of earnings, licensing, employment trends etc. High school.
Mooney Problem Checklist	The Psychological Corporation	Self report inventory used to identify problems for group discussion or individual counseling. Four Forms-junior high school to adults.
My Vocational Situation	Consulting Psychologists Press, Inc.	Provides information about one's vocational identity, occupational information, and barriers that restrict a career choice from being made. High school-adults.
New Mexico Career Education Test Series	Monitor, Inc.	Assesses specific learner objectives such as attitudes toward work and job application procedures as they relate to career education. Grades 9-12.
Occupations and Careers Information BOXSCORE	Chronicle Guidance Publications, Inc.	Measure basic knowledge of occupational information such as licensing, job entry requiremnts and occupational outlook. Grades 7-12.
Priority Counseling Survey	Minicomp Corporation	Identifies vocational and educational counseling needs. Grades 7-12 and junior college.
San Francisco Vocational Competency Scale	The Psychological Corporation	Rates mentally retarded adults for participation in sheltered workshops. Measures motor skills, cognition, responsibility, and social-emotional behavior. Mentally retarded adults.
Social and Prevocational Information Battery	CTB/McGraw-Hill	Assesses knowledge of skills regarded as important for the community adjustment of EMR students. Junior and senior high school EMR students.
Survey of Educational/ Occupational Expectations/ Aspirations	Designed Learning Association	Collects information regarding students aspirations relevant to jobs, education, marriage and career goals. Grades 7-12.
16 Personality Factors (16 PF)	Institute for Personality and Ability Testing	Assesses 16 personality dimension which can be interpreted for use in career or life adjustment counseling. Ages 16-adults.
Test for Everyday Living (TEL)	McGraw-Hill	Measures achievement in the life skills area such as banking, health care and job search skills. Jr. and Sr. high school.
Vineland Social Maturity Scale	American Guidance Services, Inc.	Interview based developmental scale which assesses an individuals ability to take responsibility and look after practical needs. Primarily mentally retarded.
Vocational Opinion Index	Associates for Research in Behavior, Inc.	Defines ones attitudes, perceptions, and motivation as they relate to the ability to obtain and maintain a job. For disadvantaged vocational trainees.

Table 2. Instruments that May Be Useful for Level III Vocational Assessment of Handicapped Students

Name	Publisher	Description & Comments on Use
Carrels for Hands On Individualized Career Education (CHOICE)	Career Research Corporation	Consists of a series of 50 self instructional carrels (job samples) designed for individual study and hands on experience. Adaptable to rehabilitation and handicapped clients.
Comprehensive Occupational Assessment and Training System (COATS)	Prep, Inc.	Consists of four components: Job matching, employability attitudes, work samples (26), and living skills. For rehabilitation clients.
Hester Evaluation System (HESTER)	Evaluation Systems, Inc.	A battery of psychological tests and ratings designed to relate client scores to the DOT. Yields 28 scores. For all IQ levels, physically handicapped and deaf.
Jewish Employment Vocational Service Work Sample System (JEVS)	Vocational Research Institute, Jewish Employment & Vocational Service	Contains 28 work samples arranged in ten DOT worker trait groups such as nut, bolt and washer assembly. For disadvantaged and other special needs people.
McCarron Dial Work Evaluation System	McCarron-Dial Systems, Common Market Press	Measures five factors: verbal-cognitive, sensory, motor, emotional and integration-coping. Utilizes eight instruments and yields 17 scores. For mentally retarded, mentally ill, learning and neurologically impaired.
Micro-Tower	ICD Rehabilitation & Research Center	A group aptitude test that uses work sample methodology to measure eight aptitudes based on the GATB. Target groups include rehabilitation, disadvantaged and special education clients.
Project Discovery	Experience Education	A career exploration package consisting of over 40 individualized simulated work situations such as masonry and sales. A guidance component is included. Ages 12-adults.
Singer Vocational Evaluation System	Singer Educational Division	Contains 25 work stations each used independently such as bench assembly, needle trades, masonry, cooking, and baking. Primarily intended for special populations.
System for Assessment and Group Evaluation (SAGE)	Progressive Evaluation Systems Corporation (PESCO)	Consists of measures of aptitude, attitude and interests related to DOT (4th edition). Not specifically designed for the handicapped, but can be used with most types of disabilities.
Systematic Approach to Vocational Evaluation (SAVE)	SAVE Enterprises	Consists of work samples designed to assess 46 worker trait groups based on the DOT. A subset of 16 worker trait group assessments are directed at the mentally handicapped and academically deprived.
Talent Assessment Program (TAP)	Talent Assessment, Inc.	Contain ten tests such as discrimination by color, gross dexterity without tools, and retention of structural and mechanical detail. For disadvantaged handicapped and emotionally disturbed.
Testing, Orientation, and Work Evaluation in Rehabilitation (TOWER)	ICD Rehabilitation & Research Center	Consists of 93 work samples arranged in 14 job training areas such as clerical, electronics assembly and mail clerk. For physically disabled as well as other handicapped persons.
Tool Tech Today	Mind, Inc.	A hands on training and assessment program in the correct and safe usage of over 100 hand tools. Non-handicapped as well as handicapped students find this system beneficial. Pre-vocational students - adults.
Valpar Component Work Sample System	Valpar Corporation	Consists of 16 work samples such as small tools, numerical sorting, money-handling and drafting. A pre-vocational readiness battery for the mentally handicapped and a perceptual abilities test for the blind are also available.
Vocational Information & Evaluation Work Sample (VIEWS)	Vocational Research Institute, Jewish Employment & Vocational Services	Consists of 16 work samples in four areas such as tile sorting, mail counting, drill press and circuit board assembly. For mild, moderate and severely retarded adults.
Vocational, Interest, Temperament and Aptitude System (VITAS)	Vocational Research Institute, Jewish Employment & Vocational Services	Consists of 21 work samples in 15 worker trait groups such as packing matchbooks, message taking, circuit board inspection and drafting. For educationally and/or culturally disadvantaged.
Vocational Skills Assessment and Development Program	Broadhead-Garrett	Consists of 3 phases with phase I containing 18 work samples based on sorting, assembly and disassembly. For handicapped and disadvantaged, ages 12-adults.
Wide Range Employment Sample Test (WREST)	Jastak Associates	Consists of ten work samples including such tasks as folding, stapling, packaging, and pattern matching. For mentally retarded, cerebral palsied, and other severely handicapped.

assessment become almost indistinguishable. However, with the help of locally developed checklists and rating sheets and a person knowledgeable in clinical observations of persons with handicaps, this type of assessment can be quite satisfactory. Even without sophisticated methods, this approach can work well when adequate supervision is available.

Job tryout is the third approach within level III assessment, and it is the least measurement-oriented of all the assessment approaches. However, it also holds the most promise for providing good data on questions concerning a person's capacity, interest, and work adjustment. It is closest to the ultimate criteria against which all other assessment must be validated; that is, a successful and satisfied employed worker. The most profitable approach to this type of assessment is through vocational cooperative education using legally constituted training agreements and training plans. Over the years, this approach to vocational education for all students, handicapped and otherwise, has been found to be most successful in placing students in jobs for which they have been trained. In this approach, the employer becomes a partner in the vocational assessment process. Moreover, evaluation data make it possible to facilitate changes in student behavior in a formative approach that shapes the student to the needs of the job while also fulfilling the student's needs.

Using Vocational Assessment Data

The IEP Process. The development of an individualized education program (IEP) for a handicapped student is an extremely important component of the career guidance and assessment process. P.L. 94–142 requires a written plan based on assessment information to be developed and implemented for every handicapped student. This plan (Office of Education, 1977) includes a statement of the student's present levels of educational performance, annual goals and short-term instructional objectives, a description of specific special education services to be provided, a statement regarding the extent of the student's participation in regular educational programs, the anticipated dates for initiation and duration of services, and evaluation criteria and procedures to be reviewed at least annually.

The team that develops the IEP consists of an agency representative qualified to provide or supervise special education (usually a school administrator); the student's teacher; the student's parents; the student, when appropriate; and other individuals at the discretion of the parent or the school. Often, schools require the receiving vocational teacher or vocational administrator to be present for considerations of vocational placement. This recommendation gives the IEP team information about entry-level competencies that the prospective student needs for successful integration into the program.

Educational Placement and Training. Based on the assessment information and the interaction of the interdisciplinary team, informed decisions about educational placement can be made. Students should be provided with a continuum of vocational educational options. The alternatives should range from placement in regular vocational programs to placement in institutional settings. To the maximum extent possible, handicapped students should be placed with nonhandicapped peers. However, if students require a more homogeneous grouping, smaller teacher-student ratio, or significantly modified vocational goals, an appropriate placement can be made in a more restrictive setting. Careful and frequent reviews should be carried out to determine whether the best decision has been made for each student.

Vocational educators who provide skills training for handicapped students should work closely with special education personnel. Support services from special education teachers can include cooperative teaching arrangements; technical assistance, such as reading examinations or teaching vocational vocabulary and concepts; development of behavioral management systems; and coordination of work study activities. Related services can include transportation, speech pathology, physical or occupational therapy, counseling, and medical and psychological services. The ultimate service, however, is a coordinated effort by professionals from two vital educational areas, special education and vocational education, to obtain occupational proficiency for handicapped students in a cooperative fashion.

Occupational Placement. After the handicapped student has mastered vocational skills in the instructional setting, occupational placement is the next step. Parnicky (1964) concludes that an ill-trained, well-placed mentally retarded employee can make a better work adjustment than a well-trained but ill-placed employee. Counselors and placement coordinators can improve chances of successful work adjustment by gathering employment information, such as work requirements, employee working conditions, hiring and firing procedures, and a map of the facilities. Campbell examines many elements of this process in Chapter Three. A clear understanding of the technical, adaptive, and social requirements of specific jobs will enable the student to begin work with confidence. Careful evaluation of the job requirements, the job site, and the student's work-related behaviors is needed. Employers can expect to teach new employees skills that they may lack, but students with special needs will not always respond to this expectation very quickly. Therefore, the special needs student is in a better position if he or she has the necessary skills prior to entering the job. When this is not possible, the cooperative education approach described in level III assessment is an excellent way of making initial placements while continuing the assessment and education process.

References

Albright, L., Evans, R. N., and Fabac, J. *A System for Identification, Assessment, and Evaluation of the Special Needs Learner.* Urbana: Bureau of Educational Research, University of Illinois, 1978.

Botterbusch, K. F. *A Comparison of Commercial Vocational Evaluation Systems.* Menomonie: Materials Development Center, Stout Vocational Rehabilitation Institute, University of Wisconsin–Stout, 1980.

Brolin, D. E., and Kokaska, C. J. *Career Education for Handicapped Children and Youth.* Columbus, Ohio: Merrill, 1979.

Clark, G. M. "Career Education: A Rationale." In G. Clark and W. White (Eds.), *Career Education for the Handicapped: Current Perspectives for Teachers.* Boothwyn, Penn.: Educational Resources Center, 1980.

Getzel, E. E., and Tindall, L. W. *Strategies for Developing a Coordinated Vocational Assessment Process for Youth.* Madison: Vocational Studies Center, University of Wisconsin–Madison, 1983.

Ginzberg, E., Ginsberg, S. W., Axelrad, S., and Herma, J. L. *Occupational Choice: An Approach to a General Theory.* New York: Columbia University Press, 1951.

Grisafe, J. P. *Vocational Assessment Handbook.* Los Angeles: Office of Riverside County Superintendent of Schools, 1983.

Hoyt, K. *Career Education, Vocational Education, and Occupational Education: An Approach to Defining Differences.* Columbus: Center for Vocational and Technical Education, Ohio State University, 1974.

Kapes, J. T., and Greenwood, K. L. "Walking the Tightrope of Student Selection." *Voc Ed Journal,* 1979, *54* (7), 24–27.

Kapes, J. T., and Mastie, M. M. *A Counselor's Guide to Vocational Guidance Instruments.* Falls Church, Va.: National Vocational Guidance Association, 1982.

Katz, M. *Decisions and Values: A Rationale for Secondary School Guidance.* New York: College Entrance Examination Board, 1963.

Krantz, G. "Vocational Evaluation in the Public Schools." In W. Pruitt (Ed.), *Readings in Work Evaluation I.* Menomonie: University of Wisconsin–Stout, 1979.

Nadolsky, J. M. "Vocational Evaluation in Public Schools: Implication for Future Practice." *Journal for Vocational Special Needs Education,* 1981, *3* (3), 5–9.

Office of Civil Rights, U.S. Department of Health, Education, and Welfare. "Vocational Education Programs Guidelines for Eliminating Discrimination and Denial of Services on the Basis of Race, Color, National Origin, Sex, and Handicap." *Federal Register,* 1979, *44* (56), 17162–17175.

Office of Education, U.S. Department of Health, Education, and Welfare. "Education of Handicapped Children: Implementation of Part B of the Education of the Handicapped Act." *Federal Register,* 1977, *42* (163), 42478.

Parnicky, J. J. "The Newly Graduated Retardate." *Rehabilitation Record,* 1964, *5* (3), 26–29.

Peterson, M. "Vocational Special Needs and Vocational Evaluation: The Needed Marriage of Two Fields." *Journal for Vocational Special Needs Education,* 1981, *3* (3), 15–18.

Salvia, J., and Ysseldyke, J. E. *Assessment in Special and Remedial Education.* Boston: Houghton Mifflin, 1978.

Sitlington, P. L. "The Assessment Process as a Component of Career Education." In G. Clark and W. White (Eds.), *Career Education for the Handicapped: Current Perspectives for Teachers.* Boothwyn, Penn.: Educational Resources Center, 1980.

Super, D. E., Crites, J. O., Hummel, R. D., Moses, H. P., Overstreet, P. L., and Warnath, C. F. *Vocational Development: A Framework for Research.* New York: Columbia University Press, 1957.

Texas Education Agency. *Guidelines for Vocational Assessment of the Handicapped.* Austin: Texas Education Agency, 1980.

Jerome T. Kapes is a professor in the vocational education program and in the department of educational psychology at Texas A & M University in College Station, Texas.

Linda H. Parrish is an associate professor of vocational education and special education and coordinator of vocational special needs programs at Texas A & M University.

Technology has changed the climate and tools of career decision making, but it takes time and talent to make these new resources work for the maximum benefit of counselors and their clients.

The Impact of Computers on Career Guidance and Assessment

Joann Harris-Bowlsbey

This chapter summarizes the impact of computers and technology on vocational guidance and assessment. The discussion will focus on software created for computers of all sizes specifically to help students and adults to enhance their own career decision making. This software includes computer-based information systems, computer-based guidance systems, and hybrids of the two. The present discussion excludes uses of the computer for data analysis, item analysis, and other functions that support vocational guidance and assessment in some way but that are not for direct use by student or client.

The term *career guidance* is used here to describe a systematic process and set of activities that individuals need to experience in order to make satisfying and informed vocational choices. The process can be learned and reused each time that a vocational choice or change occurs. Vocational assessment is a subset of this process; it involves measuring self variables relevant to vocational choice and change. Thus, vocational assessment relies on measures of interests, abilities, work-related values, competencies, and handicapped conditions.

Components of Systematic Career Guidance

The systematic process of career guidance has at least seven components. Although these components are presented sequentially here, some can occur concurrently.

R. C. Rodgers (Ed.). *Measurement Trends in Career and Vocational Education.* New Directions for Testing and Measurement, no. 20. San Francisco: Jossey-Bass, December 1983.

Component One: Development of Readiness. Development of readiness for career planning, information, and decision making can be the most difficult component. There has been very little recognition in the guidance field of the need for this component and even less research about how to develop it. Super and Overstreet (1960), Crites (1971), and Westbrook (1971) have measured degrees of readiness and identified them as elements of vocational maturity. One possible outcome of such assessment is the design of career guidance programs that provide differential treatments for individuals at different levels of readiness. This in turn could lead to criteria for measuring different effects of various methods of career guidance treatment. Mastie considers some of these questions for practitioners in Chapter One.

How can systematic, developmental, differentiated career guidance programs foster readiness or create awareness of the need to plan ahead? Research in Charles County, Maryland (Super and Bowlsbey, 1981), suggests several strategies. First, awareness should begin in the middle school years, and it is probably much more important than many of the activities currently included in career education. Second, parents have a very large role in the development of these attitudes; counselors should involve and support parents in this task. Third, time perspective or awareness of present-future relationships is a concept that grows with maturity; hence, the activities used to encourage planning must be appropriate to the age level of the learners.

New creative work is needed to design appropriate activities for the development of readiness. These activities should expand awareness of the need to plan, encourage autonomy, strengthen self-concept, and offer positive role models to enhance exploration, information seeking, and decision-making skill (Super and Bowlsbey, 1981).

Component Two: Acquisition of Relevant Self-Data. Vocational choice provides an outlet for self-variables, such as interests, abilities, and values and personality traits, but the decision maker needs to become aware of these aspects of self in an organized way. Such self-information can be acquired in at least three ways. First, a knowledgeable counselor can draw out the aspects of self and provide students and clients with structure through one-to-one interviews. Second, inventories of interests and values and batteries of aptitude tests can be administered to relate the student's or client's characteristics to national models, norm groups of similar age, or adults in specific occupations. Third, a computer can be programmed to perform the same functions as the measurement instruments by providing on-line test administration, scoring, and interpretation. The key variable in all three approaches is that linkages must be made between the individual's profile and characteristics of occupations.

Component Three: Translation of Self-Data into Information. Tiedeman (1970) distinguishes between data and information. Data are a collection of facts—in this case, facts about the self. Information is data that have been personalized so they inform the person about potential choice and paths of behavior. Starishevsky and Matlin (1963) refer to the same phenomenon as "translating psychtalk to occtalk," where *psychtalk* means a collection of fragments about the self and *occtalk* means occupational titles. The message is that any systematic career guidance program must assist the decider to link relevant self-variables (interest, skills and aptitudes, values, goals) with occupational alternatives. This implies that research must validate these linkages.

Component Four: Acquisition of Information About Identified Occupations. Information is absolutely central to the career guidance and decision-making process. Both the National Vocational Guidance Association (NVGA) and the Association of Computer-Based Systems for Career Information (ACSCI) have written guidelines for the content, accuracy, and recency of occupational information. Well-developed information is available on paper and on microfiche, through computers, and by interviewing workers in the community. Appropriate decisions clearly depend on obtaining comparable, complete, and timely information about all occupational alternatives under consideration.

Career and world-of-work information are also important. Career information refers to knowledge of life stages, their tasks, and alternative career paths or patterns. The individual needs career information to consider the lifelong process of career development and change and to understand the roles of workers in a job. World-of-work information refers to knowledge about the organization of occupations, characteristics on which they vary, and their interrelationships. This information can help individuals to understand the potential for career change. Such knowledge can ease retraining and promote the transfer of skills to new occupations throughout life. Chapters Two and Three in this volume focus on such transitions.

Component Five: Acquisition and Development of Decision-Making Skills. Acquisition and development of decision-making skills have been consistently identified by researchers as ingredients of vocational maturity. This component includes knowledge about how decisions are made and development of skills in following the steps of a systematic decision-making process. The content and skills can be taught by humans or computers directly or in simulations of the process. The goal of such instruction and simulation is to help the person to master a process that can be used again and again in all life roles. Practicing the decision-making process helps the person to learn to gather appropriate information, identify alternatives, weigh potential risks and rewards, judge how alternatives offer different combinations of satisfaction and likely success, make tentative choices, and prepare for reality testing and implementation.

Component Six: Reality Testing of Favored Alternatives. The purpose of this component is to help the person to try out alternatives as realistically as possible. Such testing can be done through simulations, courses, work study programs, jobs, internships, or practical laboratory experience. The closer these experiences are to reality, the more helpful they become to the decision-making process. Both the student and the counselor must remember that discarding unattractive alternatives is as important as selecting opportunities for further exploration. The counselor should assume the role of engineer of experience for the decider and assist in the process of creating useful reality-testing experiences. Choice should emerge from reality testing, further collection of detailed information, and clarification of the risks and benefits of each opportunity. The concept of maximizing net advantage proposed by Cassell and Rodgers in Chapter Two illustrates this challenge.

Component Seven: Implementation of Choice. Choosing an occupation always implies some next steps. These steps can include preparation to enter a college or technical school, application for financial aid, entrance into an apprenticeship or the military, or seeking and finding a job. Traditionally, counselors have provided a great deal of assistance with some of these implementation steps without paying adequate attention to the preceding components of career development and choice. Assistance with implementation should lead to specific action steps that require involvement in and commitment to a set of specific behaviors.

Types of Computer-Based Systems and Their Relationship to the Components

The process outlined in the preceding section is never finished. For most people, career development now occurs in a lifelong series of cycles through this process. Each cycle should lead the decider to a higher level of vocational maturity and healthy growth. Once decision-making skills have been learned, they can be applied again and again. The seven components of this process can be delivered to individuals by the computer alone or in combination with counseling, group guidance, curriculum, and a variety of non-computerized self-help materials.

There are several ways of assisting deciders with the career guidance process: one-to-one counseling, workshops, group guidance, curriculum, telephone service, self-help materials, and the computer. It often is best to combine the computer with one or more of these other ways.

Most computer-based systems available for lease or purchase in schools, agencies, and other settings originated at one or the other end of a continuum linking computer-based information systems with computer-based guidance systems. However, these two approaches have tended to converge over time. Systems that once represented the information end of the continuum are adding elements of the guidance process, while systems that originated at the guidance end are improving information features and local data.

Some functions are common to systems at both ends of the continuum: They store large data files, they sort and retrieve information from these files with combinations of variables, and they report detailed information about user-defined options on these variables. The files can contain information about occupations, colleges, technical schools, graduate schools, apprenticeships, military programs, financial aids, or employers. Access variables can be internal or external to the user. For example, internal variables can include interest or aptitude scores. External variables can be job characteristics, physical requirements, or related programs of study. Detailed information can consist of short summaries, responses to interactive questions, or lengthy printouts.

Computer-based systems typically vary in at least four ways: First, the typical information-emphasis system does not administer assessment instruments, such as interest inventories, ability rating scales, or values inventories at the computer terminal, although some computer-based information systems use scores or self-reports of such measures. In contrast, guidance-emphasis systems typically provide self-assessment instruments or simulations at the terminal, because they define these measures as part of the guidance process.

Second, information-emphasis systems specialize in the development of local labor market information. While guidance-emphasis systems are concerned about accurate and timely occupational information, they do not typically engage in the development of information about supply and demand in the state labor market. Instead, they tend to rely on national occupational information about work tasks, training, general employment outlook and salary ranges.

Third, information-emphasis systems typically do not use the computer to teach career development concepts, such as values clarification, organization of the world of work, the decision-making process, job-seeking skills, or life and career stages. In contrast, guidance-emphasis systems define these and related topics as central to the process approach that they attempt to enhance.

Fourth, information-emphases typically do not store individual records of use in computer files, because no long-term process is being monitored. In contrast, guidance-emphasis systems create individual computer-stored records in order to save the results of self-assessment instruments for systematic use, to prompt the client to explore parts of the system not already used, and to monitor the client's progress through the guidance process.

Computer-Based Systems and the Model

No computer-based system can replace counselors or stand entirely alone. Research (Garis, 1982; Penn, 1981) indicates that the best career guidance treatment for students combines the computer with the counselor. However, if there are not enough staff to combine such treatment, use of the computer alone produces positive and desirable effects far in excess of no treatment at all. Thus, the critical questions focus on how to divide the career guidance process among the computer, the counselor, and other strategies and resources. Table 1 summarizes the career guidance model presented earlier in this chapter and suggests how these roles can be shared. Several combinations of the two systems appear to provide more support to the guidance process

Table 1. Steps of the Career Guidance Model
in Relation to Information and Guidance Model

	Other curriculum, parents, work experience, and so forth	Computer-Based Information Systems	Computer-Based Guidance Systems	Counselor (One-to-one, group, or both)
Development of readiness for career planning, information, and decision making.	XX	—	—	XX
Acquisition of relevant self data	—	—	XX	XX
Translation of self-data into occupational alternatives	—	X	XX	XX
Acquisition of relevant information about identified occupations and related educational programs	—	XX	XX	—
Acquisition and development of decision-making skills	XX	—	XX	XX
Reality testing of favored alternatives	XX	—	—	X
Implementation of choice	—	XX	XX	X

XX = Primary responsibility
X = Secondary responsibility

than either system alone does. Myers and others (1972) support this view; their research indicates that individuals go to counselors more, not less, where computer-based systems are used. However, when a computer-based system is available, the individual relies on counselors for help in interpreting at a more professional level than information-giving alone. Counselors are also a key to efforts to develop the readiness of users for career information, decision making, and planning. Neither information systems nor guidance systems address this need, which is left for counselors who guide planned experiences in the classroom, the home, and the community.

The second component—acquisition of relevant self-data—can be shared by guidance systems and counselors. Typical computer-delivered activities can include on-line administration and interpretation of inventories of work-related values or interests and self-reported ratings of abilities or skills. One prominent career guidance system assesses interests, abilities or skills, and values, while another concentrates on values and interests. In either case, self-data are used to sort and select occupational titles for further exploration. The computer also can show the user how well his or her other interests, values, and abilities match the requirements of various occupations. Future guidance systems are likely to test abilities still more selectively so that data better than self-ratings can be acquired with a minimum of computer and user time. Computer-adaptive testing can already increase precision and decrease testing time by selecting only those items appropriate for a person's profile of skills and interests. Such interpretations can be personalized for a variety of specific combinations and delivered in a standard, objective way to each individual. Therefore, computer-adaptive guidance and testing can offer the advantages of individualized, high-quality assessment instruments, immediate scoring, and interpretive reporting.

The linkage of self-data with occupations is performed by career guidance systems and many information systems that rely on scores of assessment instruments taken on paper. The counselor also shares this role. Cassell and Rodgers offer a framework for synthesizing these elements in Chapter Two.

Both types of computer-based systems can provide excellent information about occupations targeted for exploration as well as knowledge of career and world-of-work information. As noted earlier, NVGA and ACSCI guidelines for the content, accuracy, timeliness, and scope of vocational information can help system developers to make the computer an excellent way of delivering such information in interactive question-and-answer or descriptive formats.

The computer has several significant advantages in the delivery of vocational information. First, it has high motivational appeal. Adolescents in particular prefer acquiring information by computer to acquiring it from books or microfiche. McKinlay and Adams (1971) indicate that poor readers can absorb text broken into segments and displayed on a screen considerably better than they can read the same text in printed form. In addition to its appeal in computer-delivered form, vocational information can be written and presented in a totally objective, nonbiased way without the subtle nonverbal messages that we humans sometimes transmit. Finally, computer-stored vocational information can be updated much more often than printed information can.

As already stated, component five, the acquisition or development of decision-making skills, is a hallmark of guidance systems. But there is insufficient knowledge about how decision-making skills are acquired and about how they can be taught. Nonetheless, guidance systems are attempting to make a contribution in this area through didactic teaching, computer-assisted instruction, and elements of the decision-making process. The monitoring function of the computer also can guide users through a planful process whether they are cognitively aware of it or not.

Neither information nor guidance systems are currently doing an adequate job with component six, assisting individuals with the reality testing of favored occupational alternatives. By definition, reality testing is a trial run in the real world to consider the net advantage of risks, benefits, satisfaction, or dissatisfaction. Guidance and information systems may approach this goal by the use of the videodisk, which will enable users to see and hear work settings and work tasks. But computers and videodisks will never do the whole job because simulation alone will never be enough. This component requires help from the community, the employer, and the school.

Both guidance and information systems are providing significant assistance with component seven, implementation of choice. This component involves assisting students with the next steps after they choose an occupation. These next steps involve selecting a major, a college, a graduate school, a technical school, a job, or a military program or acquiring financial aid. The different guidance and information systems vary considerably in terms of the numbers of files provided and the extent of the data that each file contains. Potentially, computers can expand the user's access to help in this area that far exceeds what the counselor alone can provide.

Benefits of Computer-Based Systems

The discussion of benefits that follows assumes that a large proportion of the material inherent in the six components proposed is being presented by the computer and the associated technology of the videodisk. Thus, the question becomes, What is or what would be the impact of delivery of career guidance and assessment services primarily by computer and associated technology in a high-tech age? The answer to this question is addressed from four perspectives by examining its impact on students and clients, counselors, program administrators, and system developers.

Impact on Students and Clients. First, users of a computer-based system gain a sense of control over their own planning. Tiedeman (1979), a pioneer in the development of computer-assisted career guidance, has suggested that the computer could be programmed to monitor an individual through a theoretically sound decision-making process. Once the user learned the process, he or she would own it and thus be in a position to apply it again and again in making life's decisions. Although this principle may appear lofty in concept, its soundness has been borne out by students who have used existing computer-based systems. Students say, "I can control what I do at the terminal," "I can go at my own speed and select those parts I want to use," and "It's a really confidential experience with no one looking over my shoulder." Thus, the computer can become a tool under the user's control. The student does not need to feel like a pawn in the hands of the counselor or advisor. The resulting feeling of autonomy and control is highly valued by users.

Second, users of computer-based systems are exposed to a broad range of options and information. The ability of counselors to assist individuals to explore vocational options is affected by their experience, their knowledge, and their prejudices or stereotypes. With good system and data file development, a computer-based system can remove all these limitations. The result is that users leave a computer-based system with a wider range of options than they might have considered alone or with counselor assistance. Further, these options can be unaffected by potential bias caused by sex, race, or irrelevant handicapping conditions. Thus, the computer can remove potential restrictive elements and motivate users to do broad exploration after leaving the computer terminal (Garis, 1982; Myers and others, 1972; Penn, 1981; Rayman and others, 1978). Students often search for and consider additional career materials, talk with people in occupations of interest, and discuss options with counselors, parents, and others based on recommendations received from computer-based information and guidance systems.

Third, users of computer-based systems experience standardized treatment. The quality of counseling personnel and the level of their expertise in the specific areas of career guidance vary widely from location to location. Further, the time that counseling personnel can allocate to delivery of career guidance services varies widely. Computer delivery assures equal access to theoretically sound career guidance and offers every user the same programmatic treatment. Delivery does not depend on counselor expertise, commitment to career guidance time, or counselor-student ratios. Assuming quality of content, it is a powerful benefit to be able to deliver a standard high-quality interpretation of assessment instruments nationwide. In a sense, it is the ultimate in quality control.

Fourth, users of computer-based systems experience personalized treatment. While I have stressed the capability of computer-based systems for standardization, it is important to note also that computer-based systems have a very real potential for personalization. Well-designed computer software allows users to select parts desired or needed at a given developmental stage or directs users to appropriate parts based on valid assessment instruments that they can take on-line. Further, measures of interest, ability, values, or vocational maturity can be interpreted differently for various categories of users based on different patterns or profiles of scores. Undoubtedly, future systems will extend personalization of computer-adaptive testing of abilities. The computer software would match tailor-made sets of items with students' strengths or weaknesses. Such adaptive modes could provide quite different items and experiences for students with different needs. This general thrust will ultimately provide test takers with the ultimate in personalization: an individualized score report and interpretation on a floppy disk.

Fifth, users of computer-based systems can experience an increase in the quantity of career guidance assistance. The national mean counselor-student ratio at the secondary level is approximately 1 to 500; at the college and university level it is 1 to 2,000; and on military posts it is 1 to 1,600. Assistance is practically nonexistent for the general adult public not in the educational setting. Counselors in each of these settings have many other duties as well. Use of the computer alone for career guidance assistance can provide many more hours of service than the counselor alone typically provides. In addition, studies (Garis, 1982; Myers and others, 1972) have indicated that use of the computer causes students and clients to request more help from counselors, not less, and that their questions are typically at a higher level of sophistication when the computer is used than when it is not. The result is that those who use computer systems get the best of both worlds — hours of assistance from the computer and hours of higher-level help from the counselor. Garis (1982) also found that students who have been encouraged free access to the computer and the counselor have sought an average of two hours with the computer and 2.33 hours with the counselors.

Another factor that affects the quantity of service relates to the new locations in which computer-based career guidance systems will be found — homes, libraries, and community learning centers. The availability of systems in these locations will increase the amount of time that users can spend. The combination of videodisk material with computer software will also expand the amount of useful material available and therefore the quantity of the time spent.

Sixth, computer-based systems increase the quality of career guidance services provided to users. All the points that have just been made add up to an improvement in the quality of career guidance services. Beyond the statements already made, however, several additional facts should be considered. First, fifteen years of research in the effectiveness of computer-based systems document such effectiveness. Use of guidance software increases knowledge of self-variables, such as interests, abilities, values, goals, and needs. Further, it increases knowledge about occupations explored at the terminal, it increases vocational maturity, and it increases specification of career plans. Finally, it promotes conversation about career planning with parents and counselors, and it stimulates career exploration in other ways.

Second, the addition of videodisk and digital voice capabilities will enable computers to appeal to alternate styles of learning — reading, hearing, and seeing combined. These same capabilities should encourage development of assessment instruments that will do a more comprehensive job of measuring abilities than paper-and-pencil methods alone can achieve. The addition of computer-adaptive testing that offers personalized, interactive, immediate feedback can greatly enhance learning and vocational maturity.

A very strong case has been made for the improvement of services to students and clients through computer-based delivery of guidance and assessment services. The overall impact seems to be highly positive. Is there any potentially negative impact? Two points appear to warrant consideration. Computer dependency may become too great. Individuals seeking career guidance may "over-believe" the machine and fail to question its logic or suggestions. Second, the general trend to use computers and related technologies for guidance, instruction, entertainment, grocery ordering, banking, and many other functions may lead interpersonal skills into atrophying. Computers cannot offer students the powerful effects of positive role models or the interaction with people who can stimulate their enthusiasm and experience in occupations of interest.

Impact on Counselors. The increasing use and the increasing capability of the computer and related technologies for career guidance and assessment will change the role of the counselor in several ways. First, the counselor will be forced to acquire some basic computer literacy in order to use the technology effectively and efficiently. Second, the counselor will need to learn to design programs in which the computer plays a very valuable role that is supplemented by positive human intervention at appropriate times. Third, the counselor will need to master a series of higher-level professional functions — managing a variety of resources and services in an optimal way for the good of students and clients. Counselors will need to address career-related questions and counseling at a more advanced level (that is, beyond information giving) and with many more clients through group delivery and self-help methods. These changes should make the counselor's role more professional. As a result, the counselor will spend more time providing in-depth counseling help to people who need one-to-one attention.

Impact on Program Administrators. The changes introduced by computer-based systems will also necessarily have an impact on career guidance program administrators. On the one hand, they will need to understand how to select and manage software licensing agreements, acquire and replace machines, and keep up with the ever changing technology. The price of hardware will continue to go down, while the cost of high-quality software will continued to rise. On the other hand, more individuals will be better served, and the per-user, per-hour cost of combined counselor and computer services will become more attractive than the cost of one-to-one service by counselors alone. Program administrators will be constantly challenged by the need to keep up with hardware developments. They will face difficult decisions as new software and hardware are introduced in the market by a variety of new developers. Administrators will have to develop criteria for choice by matching the needs of their clients with the strengths of the various systems. They will need to understand the nuances of differences across systems, the differences in guidance philosophy and quality of data, and the research base on which linkages between self-variables and occupations are made.

Impact on System Developers. As the importance of the computer as a tool for delivery of career guidance and assessment increases, developers will face some additional challenges. First, the cost of development will increase, because products will need to be converted to run on a wider variety of machines and because the number of new microcomputers and videodisk players will increase. The cost of continuing development to reach new target populations in response to competition will also be high. As greatly increased numbers of individuals use computers for career decision making, developers will assume even more responsibility for validating the linkages between search variables and occupational options and the quality of data files, producing research evidence to document claimed effectiveness, and training professionals to use the systems. All these factors will increase both the cost and the quality of available programs.

Areas for Future Research and Development

The use of the computer to assist with career guidance and development has reached the age of maturity. Research and evaluation have addressed many of the questions and concerns raised at the outset. There is now general confidence that use of computer-based systems does indeed bring positive effects to students and clients. Nonetheless, there are areas in which further work and research need to be done.

One of these areas relates to the use of assessment instruments on line that have traditionally been administered on paper. Presumably, the reliability and validity of such instruments is the same in the computer mode of delivery as it is in the paper-and-pencil mode of delivery, yet this assumption has not been tested. The assumption that individuals will get the same scores by computer administration as by paper administration also needs to be tested. The norm groups used to report interest inventory results from on-line administration have taken the instrument on paper. The whole field of adaptive testing is relatively new, and continuing research is needed to refine this very powerful capability of the computer to adjust and tailor a testing experience for each person.

Another of these areas relates to the need for more and better data about the linkage between self-variables and occupations. More research is needed on the relationship between interest inventory scores and job satisfaction, measured on self-rated abilities and job performance, and preferred values and the potential of individual occupations to attain these values. This search will be very difficult and costly.

A third area for research involves measurement of the relative effectiveness of several modes for delivery of career guidance services alone and in combination. To date, most studies have evaluated the effectiveness of the use of the computer. Some recent studies (Garis, 1982) have focused on more than one method of delivery — the computer alone, the counselor alone, and the two in combination. Still other combinations should be researched, such as the computer plus self-help material, the curriculum plus the computer, and assessment plus the computer.

A fourth area that deserves attention is longitudinal study of users of computer-based systems. All studies to date have been short-term. Some of the research questions need to focus on whether and how a decision process learned at the computer terminal is used later. Another area for investigation is whether and how use of a computer-based system helps an individual to focus vocational exploration. Does use of a computer-based system encourage a broadening of options? Do the searches of educational data files common to most systems assist an individual to identify a college or school that provides a high level of satisfaction? Are attrition and transfer minimized for students who have used computer-based systems because they have identified schools with desired characteristics? Do these students have clearer vocational goals on entry? How well does each of the lessons learned with the help of computers persist in later occupational choices and transitions?

As well as obtaining new research answers and posing new questions, future efforts should be devoted to developing new kinds of products. These products should include software for a much broader variety of assessment, programs designed for elementary and middle school children, programs to assist with adult career change, programs to assist with planning for retirement, and software designed to help a person plan for several life roles, not just the role of worker. Software of the future will be used, and therefore needs to be designed, for a much broader variety of settings. These settings will include the home, the community learning center or library, and the workplace.

References

Crites, J. O. *The Maturity of Vocational Attitudes in Adolescence.* Inquiry Series, No. 2. Washington, D.C.: American Personnel and Guidance Association, 1971.

Garis, J. "The Integrating of a Computer-Based Guidance System in a College Counseling Center: A Comparison of the Effects of DISCOVER and Individual Counseling upon Career Planning." Unpublished doctoral dissertation, Pennsylvania State University, 1982.

McKinlay, B., and Adams, D. *Evaluation of the Occupational Information Access System Used at Churchill High School.* Eugene, Ore.: Career Information System, 1971.

Myers, R. A. Lindeman, R. H., Forrest, D. J., and Super, D. E. *Educational and Career Exploration System: Report of a Two-Year Field Trial.* New York: Teachers College, Columbia University, 1972.

Penn, P. D. "Differential Effects on Vocationally Related Behaviors of Computer-Based Career Guidance System in Conjunction with Innovative Career Exploration Strategies." Unpublished doctoral dissertation, University of Minnesota, 1981.

Rayman, J. R., Bryson, D. L., and Bowlsbey, J. H. "The Field Trial of DISCOVER: A New Computerized Interactive Guidance System." *Vocational Guidance Quarterly,* 1978, *26* (349), 360.

Starishevsky, R., and Matlin, N. "A Model for the Translation of Self-Concepts into Vocational Terms." In *Career Development: Self-Concept Theory.* New York: College Entrance Examination Board, 1963.

Super, D. E., and Bowlsbey, J. H. "Planfulness in the Upper Grades: A Joint Project of Charles County Schools, Donald E. Super and JoAnn Harris-Bowlsbey." Unpublished paper, Charles County Board of Education, LaPlata, Md., 1981.

Super, D. E., and Overstreet, P. L. *The Vocational Maturity of Ninth-Grade Boys.* New York: Teachers College, Columbia University, 1960.

Tiedeman, D. V. *Third Report: Information System for Vocational Decisions.* Cambridge, Mass.: Graduate School of Education, Harvard University, 1970.

Tiedeman, D. V. *Career Development: Designing our Career Machines.* Cranston, R.I.: Carroll Press, 1979.

Westbrook, B. *Toward the Validation of the Construct of Vocational Maturity.* Technical Paper No. 6. Raleigh: Center for Occupational Education, North Carolina State University, 1971.

JoAnn Harris-Bowlsbey is assistant vice-president of the American College Testing Program and director of its DISCOVER Center, which develops and supports the computer-based career guidance software. She has been involved in the development of computer-based career guidance systems since the movement began in 1966.

*Counselors should be aware of the role of measurement in setting
and evaluating standards for entry, education, certification,
licensing, specialization, continuing education, and performance
in professional and technical occupations.*

Measurement and the Professions:
Lessons from Accounting,
Law, and Medicine

Jeri Nowakowski
Alan Nowakowski
Kathleen R. Lane

Measurement plays a significant role in selection, training, and licensing for
many occupations. Accounting, law, and medicine attract considerable interest from students, counselors, and parents because they offer many compelling
advantages. Severe competition exists for job openings in all these fields.
According to Hecker (1983), current forecasts anticipate 104,000 annual
openings in accounting and auditing, 34,000 openings per year in law, and
just 17,000 annual openings for physicians through 1990. Thus, it may be
helpful for counselors and aspiring professionals in these fields to understand
the steps in the process of becoming practitioners in accounting, law, and
medicine and in other professions that may be building on the examples that
they provide.

This chapter is divided into three parts. The first considers the role of
measurement in standard setting, entry and education, certification and licensure, specialization, and continuing education. Next, an illustrative case study
examines how a person can locate information helpful in making careful deci-

R. C. Rodgers (Ed.). *Measurement Trends in Career and Vocational Education.* New Directions
for Testing and Measurement, no. 20. San Francisco: Jossey-Bass, December 1983.

sions about entry into such professions. Finally, issues surrounding the role of measurement in these professions are addressed.

Professions and trades vary in the degree to which they try to influence the organization of their work and qualifications for membership. Accounting, law, and medicine work more actively than most professions to control selection, entry-level and continuing education, scope of practice, and ethical standards for practitioners. Thus, they are sometimes referred to as self-regulating professions. According to Schuchman and others (1981), self-regulated professions define appropriate professional behavior, help to design and implement sanctions for dealing with unethical behavior, control the organization of their work, and direct the process through which responsibility for self-regulation has been delegated by public authorities. Self-regulation is a continuous process shared with oversight agencies, courts, and state licensing boards.

Accounting, law, and medicine vary in the degree to which they self-regulate. They are examined as a group here for several reasons. First, they take more responsibility for defining sound practice and competence for their members than most other fields do. Second, self-regulation has led to measures that screen candidates and evaluate professional performance in these fields. These elements in turn have provided considerable autonomy to practitioners in these fields. Schuchman and others (1981) conclude that political changes in America have had little effect on these professional regulation systems during the past eighty years.

This chapter examines several common themes in these professions. In each, licensure and certification are complex. Details vary within and across professions and from state to state. Even within a single profession, it is difficult to find sources that synthesize the impact of standard setting, entry and education, certification and licensing, specialization, and continuing education. Major professional organizations in these fields often appear to be unaware of similarities in how people select, prepare for, and enter accounting, law, and medicine. Still more important, counselors, parents, and students are often unaware of the steps in the process of becoming a successful practitioner in licensed professions. This chapter searches for a general framework within which these issues can be examined.

How Accounting, Law, and Medicine Influence
Entry and Advancement

The practitioners of a profession can influence entry and advancement in many ways. Some of these ways are summarized for accounting, law, and medicine in Figure 1. These factors provide each profession with a decisive role in determining who may identify himself or herself as a member of the profession. They are influenced by affirmative action legislation, consumer advocacy, and state licensing boards. Nevertheless, Schuchman and others

Figure 1. Professional Avenues that Influence Entry and Advancement

	Profession		
	Accounting	Law	Medicine
Professional standard setting to define professional and sound practice	✓	✓	✓
Examinations for graduate school selection		✓	✓
Examinations to quality for licensing	✓	✓	✓
Working experience before licensure (apprenticeship)			✓
Continuing professional education	✓	✓	✓
Professional disciplinary mechanism	✓	✓	✓
Professionally required graduate programs		✓	✓
Specialization certification			✓

(1981) conclude that entry into these professions continues to be controlled primarily by members of these professions.

The influence that a profession has on its membership is both cumulative and interactive. Figure 2 displays five areas of influence. Standards of performance must be defined before valid measures can be developed. Standard setting relies on generally accepted principles of practice, which guide measurement, the content of training programs, and performance standards. These in turn help to define the logical content of examinations for licensure and, in the medical specialty areas, for certification. Continuing education allows a profession to update and evaluate its members. Research and feedback from entry exams, preparatory training, licensing, certification, and continuing education can help to refine definitions of sound practice, competence, and training over time.

Figure 2.

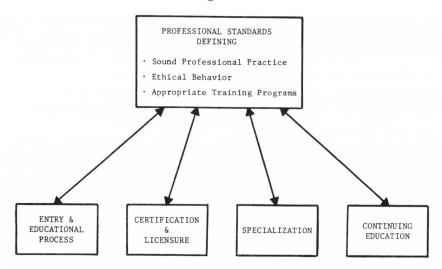

Professional Standard Setting. Perhaps the most fundamental method of control for a profession is its legal right and responsibility to set standards that define sound practice (Wheat and others, 1972). Recognition and definition of performance standards then provide structure for entry-level and continuing education, licensure tests, accreditation and peer reviews, and performance assessments. Controls over professions that serve the public welfare are intended to protect the health, safety, and financial security of individuals. These professions may be regulated externally if the public welfare is an issue and if meaningful professional standards are not available to determine practical ways of measuring and evaluating performance. One characteristic that distinguishes accounting, law, and medicine from most other fields is the active role that practitioners take in defining sound, ethical practice for themselves and their training programs.

One significant measure of a profession's autonomy is the amount of external control exerted by the courts and agencies of government. For example, while the Securities and Exchange Commission (SEC) has been empowered since its creation in 1933 to set standards for accounting, it delegates that responsibility to the Financial Accounting Standards Board (FASB) and the Auditing Standards Board (ASB). The American Institute of Certified Public Accountants (AICPA) in turn houses the ASB and monitors professional standards through its code of professional ethics, the uniform certified public accountant (CPA) examination, and other measures such as peer review to assure that these standards are met (American Institute of Certified Public Accountants, 1982). The SEC then monitors these efforts with the help of other responsible government agencies and congressional subcommittees.

Candidates should know how such standards relate to educational preparation and licensing. A commitment to prepare for a career in one of these fields should be based on careful assessment of the benefits and requirements of meeting entry and performance standards in a profession. For example, contrast the route that one might take to become a mathematics teacher or a certified public accountant. AICPA, the largest but not the only professional organization in accounting, develops the uniform CPA examination and is therefore a logical source of information. Candidates may then be referred to a state CPA society or licensing board for additional information about requirements in a particular state. However, there should be substantial similarity in the information regardless of the source, because most state variations occur within the guidelines set by the accounting profession, which are uniformly assessed by the national AICPA examination.

Finding out how to become a mathematics teacher is less direct. While the National Education Association and the American Federation of Teachers offer advisory professional standards, no uniform national examination defines the entry-level knowledge required to teach mathematics. State teacher certification boards sometimes require the National Teacher Examination, but some of the major teacher organizations have resisted the use of tests in this process. All states require a minimum number of appropriate college courses in mathematics and education, including a brief student teaching or internship experience. However, substantial variations are permitted in the content of teacher preparation programs, courses of instruction, and entry requirements. University mathematics and education faculty also share responsibility for defining courses of study. Finally, local school districts hire and evaluate mathematics teachers without uniform standards to define exemplary or substandard performance.

The presence of multiple sets of standards affect entry and advancement in any field. Professions that are actively involved in setting standards to govern their practice and membership are more likely than others to control training and measurement of professional performance in the field. While standard setting does not guarantee direct control over these activities, certainly the absence of a systematic method for defining entry-level and performance requirements in a profession invites intervention — a factor that may be important to the teaching profession in the current national debate about excellence in the schools.

A profession that actively engages in standard setting should have a documented standard-setting rationale and a history of refining that rationale to maintain its authority; visible standard-setting bodies actively reviewing, interpreting, and refining standards; documentation available to the public and useful for professionals; and evidence that standards are being used to guide education, accreditation, licensure, peer review, professional disciplinary efforts, and so on (Ridings, 1980).

In accounting, law, and medicine, sound professional practice is defined by the professions, but it is monitored and interpreted by public oversight and licensing agencies. For example, accounting standards are set by the FASB, and auditing standards are set by the ASB. General understanding of professional standards is assessed in the uniform CPA exam. Professional standards are also referred to daily by practicing accountants and auditors. The profession plays a key role in program accreditation and peer review standards through the AICPA.

Ethical standards for attorneys are produced by the American Bar Association (ABA), and in most states they are covered on the bar exam. Accreditation standards, which the ABA has issued since 1921, influence the content of law school programs. Standards for training are likewise monitored through program accreditation in law and medicine. Standards for medical professionals are generated by peer review to determine appropriate practice and they are continually reviewed and refined to remain abreast of developments in technology and research. Medical specialty boards play an increasing role in setting standards for graduate medical education and specialty practice.

The first step in finding reliable information is to determine who decides what the members of a profession should know and how they should practice. In accounting, law, and medicine, those determinations are largely the work of the professional groups. This makes the major organizations in each profession—the AICPA, the ABA, and the American Medical Association (AMA)—excellent places in which to begin learning about how to prepare for entry and success in accounting, law, or medicine.

The Entry and Education Process. As every chapter in this volume emphasizes, entry into a profession is more a process than a single event. Education plays a major role in that process, and measurement provides part of the information that controls access to education, as Figure 3 shows. In all three fields, preparation to become a professional begins with high school. Entry into undergraduate programs, such as premed or accounting, depends on the combined influence of performance on the Scholastic Aptitude Test (SAT), high school grades, difficulty of the course work completed, and rank in class. Near the end of college undergraduate studies, students interested in law or medicine typically take the Law School Admissions Test (LSAT) or the Medical College Admissions Test (MCAT). Accounting majors typically take the CPA exam during their last year of undergraduate study or during their first few years of professional practice.

Norm-referenced standardized tests play an important role in determining entry into a profession, because they help to determine admission into college, graduate education, professional membership or licensing, and, in some cases, specialization. Additionally, criterion-referenced testing is a major element in college preparatory programs and graduate education. In medicine, students are also evaluated during their applied training at hospitals and health centers. Tests are and should continue to be only one of the factors in these decisions in combination with grades, coursework, honors received, and predictions by professionals of performance in graduate training. The AMA's

Figure 3. Measures Used at Critical Points Prior to Attaining Professional Licensure

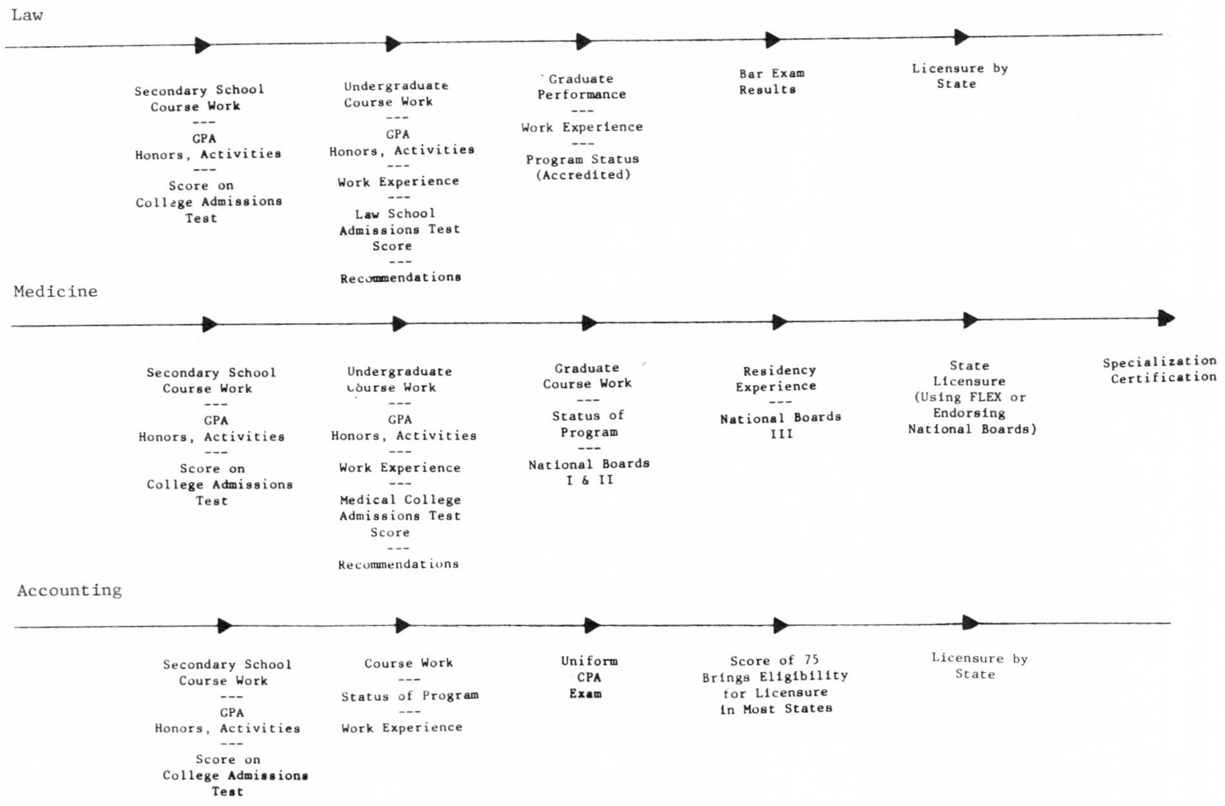

Law

Secondary School Course Work

GPA
Honors, Activities

Score on College Admissions Test

Undergraduate Course Work

GPA
Honors, Activities

Work Experience

Law School Admissions Test Score

Recommendations

Graduate Performance

Work Experience

Program Status (Accredited)

Bar Exam Results

Licensure by State

Medicine

Secondary School Course Work

GPA
Honors, Activities

Score on College Admissions Test

Undergraduate Course Work

GPA
Honors, Activities

Work Experience

Medical College Admissions Test Score

Recommendations

Graduate Course Work

Status of Program

National Boards I & II

Residency Experience

National Boards III

State Licensure (Using FLEX or Endorsing National Boards)

Specialization Certification

Accounting

Secondary School Course Work

GPA
Honors, Activities

Score on College Admissions Test

Course Work

Status of Program

Work Experience

Uniform CPA Exam

Score of 75 Brings Eligibility for Licensure in Most States

Licensure by State

Council on Medical Education (1982, p. 7) has noted that there is "no evidence available on relationships between performance on the MCAT and subsequent performance as a practitioner, educator, or researcher." However, testing still continues to play a role in comparing and selecting highly competitive candidates for limited openings in all three fields. Preparation for each of these professions requires the ability to perform successfully in rigorous academic training and licensure examinations, both of which are related to scores on the SAT, the MCAT, or the LSAT (Council on Medical Education, 1982; American Bar Association, 1982; Leathers and others, 1982). As a result, all three professions continue to invest in efforts to enhance the validity of selection measures as predictors of performance in training.

Certification and Licensure. While a professional license to practice seems a long way off to the high school student, early knowledge of licensing requirements can help aspiring professionals to make important decisions about where and what to study. Measurement, particularly testing, plays a pivotal role in the certification and licensing process in all three professions.

Licensing is a process through which a state or other agency of government grants permission to an individual to practice after the person has met standards of competence required to protect public health, safety, and welfare (Public Health Services, 1977). Certification is primarily a quality control tool for a profession. According to Shimberg (1981), certification helps the public to identify practitioners who have met a professional standard well above that set by licensure alone. In contrast, accreditation focuses on assuring that training programs meet prescribed standards and prepare students to satisfy performance and ethical standards in the profession.

Certification and licensure are essentially synonymous in law. In medicine and accounting, they are different processes, although certification is less developed in accounting than it is in the medical specialties. For example, board-certified medical specialists, such as surgeons, neurologists, and pediatricians, meet standards set by private specialty societies beyond those required to obtain a license to practice medicine in a state. More than twenty such boards are affiliated with the American Board of Medical Specialties. In addition to the CPA, accounting offers certification in Management Accounting from the National Association of Accountants and certification in Internal Auditing from the Institute of Internal Auditors. In each case, certification is voluntary.

All three professions rely on formal testing, as Figure 4 shows. The uniform CPA exam qualifies an individual to apply for state licensure to practice as a certified public accountant. The examination is given in May and November of each year over a two and a half day period; it includes a one-day section in accounting practice, plus half-day sections in accounting theory, business law, and auditing. Just 15 percent pass all four sections on the first try, about 25 percent pass one to three parts, and at least 50 percent typically receive no credit at all (Leathers and others, 1982). Between 70 and 85 percent

Figure 4. Overview of Examinations Used for Licensure in Accounting, Law, and Medicine

Profession	Major Test(s) Used for Licensure	Prerequisites for Taking	Type of Test	Pass-Fail Ratio	Cutoff Standards
Accounting	Uniform CPA exam	In most states, a B.A. degree from a college recognized by the board; a specified number of credit hours of accounting and related subjects	Three-day (19.5 hour) four-part test; multiple-choice, essay, or problem-type questions; each section is 60 percent multiple-choice, 40 percent essay or problem-type.	15 percent pass rate for first-time takers passing all sections; eventual 75 percent pass rate	Score of 75 on exam (can vary by state but is stable)
Law	Multistate Bar Exam and additional portions Multistate Professional Responsibility Exam	In most states, graduation from an accredited law program.	200-question six-hour test; essay tests over state laws Multiple-choice test on Code of Professional Responsibility	Fluctuates by state (for example, 50.2 percent in California, 91.7 percent in Texas, 77 percent in Michigan in 1980)	Fluctuates by state; passing scores must range between 115 and 150
Medicine	National Boards I, II, and III Federation Licensing Exam (FLEX)	Graduation from an accredited medical program; residency experience Graduation from medical program (can include foreign programs)	Parts I and II: two-day multiple-choice tests; part III: one-day exam on diagnosis, patient management Three-day multiple-choice test	In 1982, 82 percent pass part I, 98 percent pass part II, 98 percent pass part III In 1981, 55 percent pass	Passing score determined by norm-referenced group; relatively stable range In most states, a weighted average of 75

of those who try again eventually complete all four parts of the exam within five years (Lodge, 1977).

In medicine, two routes are available to meet state licensing requirements. Most students in American medical colleges take examinations prepared by the National Board of Medical Examiners (NBME). These tests, known as the National Boards, are milestones in the medical education of aspiring physicians. The first part, a two-day exam, focuses on basic medical sciences, such as anatomy, behavioral sciences, biochemistry, microbiology, pathology, pharmacology, and physiology. The first part, which was passed by 84 percent of the candidates who took it in 1981, is often required for promotion from the second to the third year of medical school. The second part, a two-day test measuring knowledge in the clinical sciences, such as internal medicine, pediatrics, psychiatry, and surgery, is required in some schools for promotion to later stages of medical training. In 1981, 97.5 percent of those who took the second part passed it. The candidate takes the third part after receiving the M.D. degree. The third part assesses patient management skills and the ability to diagnose medical problems in simulations of real clinical situations. Nationally, 98 percent passed the third part in 1981.

The second route to licensure as a physican is the FLEX, a three-day test made up of items from all three parts of the National Boards. In 1981, 55 percent of the candidates passed the FLEX. Each year, 75 percent of U.S. medical graduates are licensed with scores from the National Boards. While the National Boards are longer than the FLEX, candidates for the boards can complete the first two parts soon after they finish medical and clinical science courses, when the knowledge is still fresh. In addition, students can prepare for each part of the National Boards separately.

In all but two states, candidates who wish to be admitted to legal practice must pass a written bar examination. Most states require graduation from an ABA-accredited law program and rely on the Multistate Bar Examination, which covers material applicable to all states. In addition, most states require a day-long essay test in which candidates apply state law to a series of complex problems. Recently, some states have added the Multistate Professional Responsibility Examination to these requirements. However, since cutoff scores can vary, candidates who take the same tests can get different results depending on the standards that prevail in a particular state.

Graduation from accredited training programs is usually required for eligibility to take licensing exams in medicine and law, and the AICPA is considering recommendations for such a standard for accounting. Thus, accreditation is linked directly to licensing in these professions. Accreditation is essentially a self-regulatory evaluation process to influence the quality of professional training programs. Lists of accredited programs are available from professional associations and their state societies.

Licensing requirements in all three professions vary across states. There tends to be more variance in law than in accounting or medicine. However, some states (Hawaii, for example) require a master's degree and one year of practical experience to qualify candidates for taking the CPA exam. Other states require a bachelor's degree and as much as two years of experience. Thus, a student is wise to study differences in licensing requirements and pass-fail rates in particular states of interest.

Continuing Education. Continuing education is one means of assuring the public that licensed professionals continue to perform competently. Eventually, examinations may recertify some professionals and monitor how well they have maintained their skills and knowledge (Schuchman and others, 1981; Shimberg, 1981). The National Board of Family Practice and the National Commission on the Certification of Physicians' Assistants already require periodic reexamination for continued certification. The AICPA directory (American Institute of Certified Public Accountants, 1982, p. iv) states that "a CPA must periodically apply for certificate renewal" and keep up with professional developments through continuing education. Such training is mandatory in forty-five states (Commerce Clearing House, 1982, p. 151).

Since the 1970s, accounting, law, and medicine have all initiated mandatory continuing education in revisions of their professional standards. Forty-five states require continuing education for accountants, and nine states have mandated such training for lawyers (Schuchman and others, 1981). Eighteen states have continuing medical education requirements for membership renewal in state medical societies, for reregistration, or to qualify for malpractice self-insurance plans ("Continuing Medical Education Fact Sheet," 1983). In addition, many professional societies and associations help practitioners to meet these requirements by organizing national programs and meetings to promote continuing education among their members.

Continuing education can serve a number of self-regulating purposes: It can update professionals in new content and skill areas; it can monitor and remedy problems in professional practice (for example, a state society can require continuing education for a professional brought before a disciplinary board); it can educate practitioners in specialized areas; and it can protect the public from professionals who do not perform ethically or competently.

Issues in continuing education include cost, quality control, and the measurement of impact and effectiveness. Evaluation of continuing education in law and accounting is relatively difficult, because there is no single, formal process for its accreditation. In medicine, the accreditation process is tightly controlled by state societies, medical specialty societies, and the Accreditation Council for Continuing Medical Education. Where there has been resistance to end-of-course testing for evaluation, the lack of national accreditation standards for most continuing education programs have made effective measures of the impact of these programs difficult to gather.

The aspiring professional in these fields should assume that continuing education will be part of professional life. Continuing education may help to reduce the demand for professional recertification exams proposed by some federal agencies and consumer advocates. Continuing education can be tailored to a professional's needs through individual audits and computer-assisted course work. However continuing education is delivered, measurement of its impact will continue to be important in monitoring its quality and in justifying its costs.

Specialization. Many young people declare their interest in medicine by selecting a specialty first, such as pediatrics or surgery. Just as professions influence entry, specialty areas also define their own criteria for entry and performance. Specialization adds another round of preparation, training, and certification to the process.

More than twenty major specialty areas exist in medicine, and there are subspecialties in several of these areas. While details vary, certification in a specialty generally requires about five years of postgraduate training and experience in the specialty field, followed by comprehensive examinations to become board-certified.

Most states are either considering or have already adopted specialization plans for attorneys, but such plans vary greatly. In some states, lawyers can identify themselves as specialists without examination. Where formal certification plans exist, they call for oral and written examinations and experience in the area of specialty. The ABA has offered a model for specialization that calls for a Board of Legal Specialization to act as the governing body (Schuchman and others, 1981).

The situation in accounting is less clear. The most recent data from the U.S. Department of Labor (Bureau of Labor Statistics, 1982) indicate that there are more than 200,000 CPAs, 20,000 licensed public accountants, and about 10,000 certified internal auditors among the 887,000 persons who worked as accountants and auditors in 1980. In addition, larger accounting and auditing firms can offer areas of specialty in work assignments, such as expertise in a particular industry or in computer-assisted auditing techniques. Thus, while certified subspecialties do not currently exist in most areas of accounting, specialization is among the issues under study in the profession.

Two measurement issues are part of the debate over specialization. The first is whether one-time certification exams are effective in maintaining competence. Should professionals be reexamined, and how often, and what should the consequences be if they fail? Second, more data is needed on the general effects of specialization—its value in refining existing specialties, in defining new ones, in assessing the relative costs and benefits of small and large practices, in improving the quality of services or the competence of practicing professionals.

Planning to Become a CPA

One way to consider the process of preparing for and meeting professional standards is to trace the process that a person goes through. The illustrative case that follows is offered for the consideration of counselors, students, and others interested in this process.

Susan had always been good in math. She especially liked adding up numbers in her head and solving number games and puzzles. Recently, she overheard two people in a restaurant talking about a merger of two companies. It sounded complicated, but they kept referring to a key person whom they called a *CPA*. Susan wasn't sure who or what that was, but it sounded interesting, and she wanted to know more. She decided to ask for help.

The next day, she asked her counselor at school what a CPA does. The counselor reached for the *Occupational Outlook Handbook* (Bureau of Labor Statistics, 1982). It told her what a CPA does. It also indicated that one must pass a very difficult test in order to become a CPA. The handbook suggested writing to the American Institute of Certified Public Accountants for information about careers in accounting.

With help from her counselor, Susan wrote to the AICPA. The counselor also advised Susan to check the local library for more information while she was waiting for a response to her letter. When she did, Susan was surprised to find several books on the topic. One (Rosenthal, 1978) was written by a CPA, while another (Lodge, 1977) was by a man who worked for the AICPA. Both authors offered advice about what a good accountant needs: a "feel for figures," not a strong interest in advanced math; the ability to express oneself well in speaking and writing, especially to explain complicated numbers clearly and simply; and an outgoing, gregarious, self-assured approach with "a liking for new, challenging situations, a readiness to innovate and lead, and an interest in working with others" (Lodge, 1977, p. 21).

All of these characteristics increased Susan's interest. She wanted to work with people and with numbers. She was also intrigued by the advice that such college preparatory courses as languages, mathematics, and science "may be a better foundation for accounting training in college than high school business subjects. English is most important" (Lodge, 1977, p. 23).

A few weeks later, Susan received several booklets from the AICPA, including *Information for CPA Candidates* (American Institute of Certified Public Accountants, 1983), which told her about the CPA exam and which said that each state sets its own requirements that a person must meet in order to take the test. Lodge (1977) and Rosenthal (1978) both listed names and addresses of state boards of accountancy. She decided to write to the board in her state, which told her that she would need a four-year degree from a college or university program approved by the state board plus a specified number of credit hours of accounting and related subjects before she could take the uniform CPA exam. She found that several schools in her state were among the 146 colleges in forty-five states that, Lodge (1977) indicated, were approved by the American Assembly of Collegiate Schools of Business (AACSB). Each of these schools proved to be on her state accountancy board's list of approved college accounting programs.

Susan was pleased to read that opportunities for accountants and auditors were expected to grow faster than the average for all occupations through 1990 and that 43 percent of the candidates sitting for the exam in 1981 were women (McInnes and MacNeill, 1983, p. 3). Based on the information that she received from several sources, Susan began going to the public library's business reading room to look at magazines from some of the accounting associations that she had read about. She found the AICPA's *Journal of Accountancy* and the National Association of Accountants's (NAA) *Management Accounting*. While browsing in the business reading room one afternoon, she discovered the AICPA directory (American Institute of Certified Public Accountants, 1982). It listed several firms and accountants in her city. As she scanned the list, she was surprised to discover that the father of one of her classmates was a senior partner with a major accounting firm. When she called to ask whether he would be willing to talk with her, Susan was invited to spend a day in his office and to join in a meeting of the local chapter of the NAA.

Susan was well on her way to knowing the requirements that she would have to meet in order to qualify as an accountant, auditor, or financial analyst or as a candidate for one of the many other careers related to accounting. With a lot of her own initiative and a little help from her counselor, she had begun to meet people and find resources that would be of help to her in any career decision, regardless of whether she changed her mind later about preparing to become a CPA.

Learning from the Professions

Vocational counselors and candidates can best assess the candidates' chances for successful entry and performance in accounting, law, and medicine when they know the criteria recommended by the profession for selection, the number and nature of measures used to evaluate candidates on these criteria, and the importance assigned to criteria in various states and specialties. Testing plays an important role in the process of training and licensure in accounting, law, and medicine, so both candidates and counselors should be familiar with the examinations and with their part in these professions.

In all three professions, major professional organizations provide information about screening and licensing exams. Undergraduate training needs to be selected with sensitivity to professional training and knowledge likely to be required to enter medical or law schools for those who wish to pursue these professions. Demographic and testing data from professional organizations often display such differences. Two examples are American Bar Association (1982) and Leathers and others (1982) from the AICPA. Additional information is available from professional organizations and state licensing boards, and books and programs offering coaching and independent study.

The most critical measurement issue is validity. Do selected measures identify and measure the qualities that are important in producing competent professionals? Shimberg (1981) has argued that the tests used for licensing should be able to identify persons with the skills and abilities to perform in a way that will safeguard the public welfare. In contrast, certification tests should indicate whether someone has met prescribed professional standards of competence. Neither kind of test, Shimberg maintains, is intended to predict job success. Further, given the diversity of practice situations to which newly licensed and certified professionals are exposed, Shimberg suggests that it may not be technically feasible to do a criterion-related validity study of a licensing or certifying exam.

Nevertheless, there is evidence that all three professions are concerned with the validity of measures used to screen candidates both for professional education and for licensure. For instance, accounting invests substantial resources in practice analysis surveys in which practitioners confidentially respond to detailed questionnaires regarding how they spend their time. Documented priorities are then used to validate content areas on the CPA exam. Additionally, *Information for CPA Candidates* (American Institute of Certified Public Accountants, 1983) describes the rigorous system for grading CPA exams.

Medicine is promoting a broader education for professionals and the use of multiple criteria and measures for selection, training, and continuing education (Council on Medical Education, 1982, pp. 6–7): "Medical schools should require their admissions committees to make every effort to determine that the students admitted possess integrity as well as the ability to acquire the knowledge and skills required of a physician. . . . Continuing review of admissions tests is encouraged, because the subject content of such examinations has an influence on premedical education and counseling." Similarly, the ABA (American Bar Association, 1982, p. 59) urges: "Public authority should continually strive to make its methods of examination more effective so that the results will be the nondiscriminatory admission of none not qualified and the exclusion of none qualified, even though this requires the use of innovative examining techniques and constant consideration of the ever changing needs of our society. The necessity to train lawyers to represent all members of society is a continual challenge to teachers of law and legal education. To test this properly the examining authority can perform effectively and satisfactorily only if it makes responsive changes in its techniques."

Thus, all three professions profoundly influence the nature of their membership. They do so by committing to definitions of standard and substandard performance that permit the development and use of reasonable measures. The validity of measures used for screening and licensing is, and should be, of concern in each profession. Selected measures must continually be studied and refined so that they play a valid role in selecting and advancing the most qualified candidates. Proper use of measures by state licensing boards must also be promoted.

Perhaps the most impressive lesson provided by accounting, law, and medicine deals with professional responsibility. The influence that these professions exert in determining both the organization of their work and the nature of their membership comes at no small cost of professional resources. Further, the accountability trail is much easier to follow in these professions. Justifications for and explanations of the influential role that they play are unending. Their example makes it clear that increased professional influence is purchased at the cost of increased professional responsibility. This is a lesson that many professional fields must still learn and one that accounting, law, and medicine must continue to remember.

References

American Bar Association. *A Review of Legal Education in the United States, 1981–82: Law School and Bar Admission Requirements*. Chicago: American Bar Association, 1982.

American Institute of Certified Public Accountants. *Accounting Firms and Practitioners*. New York: American Institute of Certified Public Accountants, 1979.

American Institute of Certified Public Accountants. *Information for CPA Candidates*. (6th ed.) New York: American Institute of Certified Public Accountants, 1983.

Ayers, J. (Ed.). *Continuing Medical Education Fact Sheet*. Chicago: American Medical Association, 1983.

Bureau of Labor Statistics, U.S. Department of Labor. *Occupational Outlook Handbook, 1982–83 Edition*. Washington, D.C.: U.S. Government Printing Office, 1982.

Commerce Clearing House. *Accountancy Law Reporter*. Chicago: Commerce Clearing House, 1983, supplemented monthly.

Council on Medical Education, American Medical Association. *Future Directions for Medical Education*. Chicago: American Medical Association, 1982.

Hecker, D. E. "A Fresh Look at Job Openings." *Occupational Outlook Quarterly*, 1983, *27* (2), 27–29.

Leathers, P. E., Sullivan, J. A., and Bernstein, J. *Uniform Statistical Information Questionnaire: 1980*. New York: American Institute of Certified Public Accountants, 1982.

Lodge, A. *Opportunities in Accounting*. Louisville, Ky.: Vocational Guidance Manuals, 1977.

McInnes, M., and MacNeill, J. H. *The Supply of Accounting Graduates and the Demand for Public Accounting Recruits, 1983*. New York: American Institute of Certified Public Accountants, 1983.

Public Health Services, U.S. Department of Health, Education and Welfare. *Credentialing Health Manpower*. Publication no. 05–77–50057. Washington, D.C.: U.S. Government Printing Office, 177.

Ridings, J. M. "Standard Setting in Accounting and Auditing: Considerations for Educational Evaluation." Unpublished doctoral dissertation. Western Michigan University, 1980.

Rosenthal, L. *Your Future in Accounting Careers*. New York: Richard Rosen Press, 1978.

Schuchman, H. L., Abel, E., and Frampton, S. *Self-Regulation in the Professions: Accounting, Law, Medicine*. Washington, D.C.: National Science Foundation, 1981.

Shimberg, B. "Testing for Licensure and Certification." *American Psychologist*, 1981, *36* (10), 1138–1146.

Wheat, F. M., Biegler, J. C., Levin, A. I., Olson, W. E., Pryor, T. C., Smith, R. B., and Solomon, D. *Establishing Financial Accounting Standards*. New York: American Institute of Certified Public Accountants, 1972.

Sources of Additional Information

American Institute of Certified Public Accountants. *Uniform CPA Examination, November 1982; Questions and Unofficial Answers.* New York: American Institute of Certified Public Accountants, 1983.

This AICPA booklet offers information and unoffical answers for the November 1982 uniform CPA examination.

American Medical Association. *Helping Hands: Horizons Unlimited in Medicine.* (3rd ed.) Chicago: American Medical Association, 1981.

This fact book describes educational requirements and career opportunities in medicine. It can be purchased from Order Department, OP-160, American Medical Association, P.O. Box 821, Monroe, Wis. 53566.

Law School Admissions Council. *Prelaw Handbook.* Newton, Pa.: Association of American Law Schools, 1982.

This handbook discusses prelaw and law study and includes a two-page summary of each law school.

Strickland, R. *How to Get into Law School.* New York: Hawthorn Books, 1977.

The author discusses law school admissions offices and policies and offers suggests for planning undergraduate curriculum and applying to law school.

Jeri Nowakowski is an assistant professor at Northern Illinois University in the Department of Leadership and Education Policy Studies. Research on this chapter was completed during a postdoctoral fellowship in the Division of Methodology and Evaluation research at Northwestern University.

Alan Nowakowski is an evaluation analyst in the Professional Education Division of Arthur Andersen & Co., where he is responsible for coordinating evaluation studies of the impact of training on job performance and organizational productivity.

As a professional associate at the Midwestern office of Educational Testing Service, Kathleen R. Lane directed research studies for K-12 schools and gave technical assistance for evaluating school programs.

Helping people make wise choices about and commitments to work is a challenge worthy of all the attention and resources we can find.

Concluding Synthesis

Ronald C. Rodgers

This volume of *New Directions for Testing and Measurement* examines the issues surrounding the lifelong process of occupational choice and commitment. The authors examine how students and job seekers make such choices, how counselors and others can help, how successful adaptation to particular jobs happens, how persons with special needs can experience success, how computers complement the efforts of people and add to the resources available to help the indivividual student and job seeker, and how professions regulate and assess entry and performance.

Many of the insights presented in this volume build on several common assumptions: that the opportunities available to a person are the result of choices and decisions accumulated over many years rather than a single, monumental event; that each person can, and many do, change occupations as new skills are acquired and changes occur in the labor market; that each person can create unique combinations of his or her talents, needs and interests, and match them to the requirements of particular jobs, industries, and employers.

The toughest task for counselors may be to convince the student and job seeker that new choices and opportunities can result from decisions to acquire new skills. A person must prepare for luck and the good will of others to be ready for new challenges and opportunities when they occur. Some people are satisfied to rely mainly on luck, but those who want to share in the control of such events must be willing to take full responsibility for their own

R. C. Rodgers (Ed.). *Measurement Trends in Career and Vocational Education.* New Directions for Testing and Measurement, no. 20. San Francisco: Jossey-Bass, December 1983.

choices about work to avoid the plight of Sylvia Plath's (1971, pp. 84–85) heroine, who imagined herself sitting in a fig tree loaded with fruit. Each fig represented a wonderful future, but she saw herself "starving to death, just because I couldn't make up my mind which of the figs I would choose. I wanted each and every one of them, but choosing one meant losing all the rest, and, as I sat there, unable to decide, the figs began to wrinkle and go black, and, one by one, they plopped to the ground at my feet."

Choice is the first requirement, but choice must then be followed by sustained commitment to gaining skill and experience on which to build future choices and opportunities. This process is repeated each time a person enters or leaves a job, an occupation, an industry, training, or other preparation for future opportunities. Only the individual who must implement each step in a personal career development plan can take full responsibility for these decisions. Counselors, parents, and others can help, but each person must have full ownership of his or her career plan in order to make it happen.

Thus, occupational choice is a lifelong process of assessing and balancing the risks and benefits of each opportunity we encounter. Tests can serve as checkpoints as each person progresses through recurrent cycles of exploration, entry, adaptation, and transition in various occupations from local to international labor markets. There are no magic pathways or formulas that assure success, and very few deadends. Each person is challenged to create opportunities that match his or her needs, talents, and interests. A good match is usually the result of a lot of hard work and being ready when the right opportunity becomes available, but the rewards of finding a satisfying job can be unlimited.

There is little doubt that the investment in preparing for satisfying occupational choices and commitments is warranted. The key is not so much what a person chooses or prepares for, but *that* each person chooses, sustains a commitment long enough to learn from and build on it, and adapts his or her talents in response to opportunities that emerge as job requirements and labor markets change.

The challenge to the individual student and job seeker is to make wise choices and commitments. The challenge to the counselor, parent, and others who wish to help is to assure that testing and assessment add insight and knowledge to the process. It is an endlessly demanding and rewarding opportunity for us all.

Reference

Plath, S. *The Bell Jar.* New York: Harper, 1971.

Index